This should be returned
Library

D0411325

ONE OF LOWRY'S CHILDREN

ONE OF LOWRY'S CHILDREN

A PERSONAL MEMOIR

TERRY MAHER

QUARTET

First published in 2015 by Quartet Books Limited
A member of the Namara Group
27 Goodge Street, London W1T 2LD
Copyright © Terry Maher 2015
The right of Terry Maher to be identified
as the author of this work has been asserted
by him in accordance with the
Copyright, Designs and Patents Act, 1988
All rights reserved.
No part of this book may be reproduced in
any form or by any means without prior
written permission from the publisher
A catalogue record for this book
is available from the British Library
ISBN 978 0 7043 7401 0
Typeset by Josh Bryson

Printed and bound in Great Britain by
International Ltd, Padstow, Cornwall

LANCASHIRE COUNTY LIBRARY	
3011813315944 6	
Askews & Holts	03-Feb-2016
324.24106 MAH	£20.00
HRA	

This memoir is dedicated to the mother I lost nearly 70 years ago; the mother I hardly knew

By Terry Maher

Against My Better Judgement
Unfinished Business
Counterblast (with Dennis Wrigley & Alan Share)
Grumpy Old Liberal
What Would a Liberal Do?

CONTENTS

I
94 VIADUCT STREET

I have very few memories of my mother, which is not helpful when writing a memoir. I find this surprising, as I was 11 when she died and might have been expected to have remembered more. Only one photograph remains, but she was already sick at the time and I am told that it is not a fair representation. I find it difficult to bring to mind her features and how she was about the house; how she spoke, her tone, her vocabulary; she will certainly have had a strong Manchester accent. And I cannot remember a hug, or a kiss, or a smile. Yet I know that she was both warm and affectionate and a loving mother to her two boys.

Lilian Redman was born in 1914 to a Protestant family living in Ancoats close to the centre of Manchester. Her family was not noticeably religious, rarely seeing the inside of a church, but that did not make it any less bigoted. It might seem odd to emphasise this point, but religious persuasion was usually the only distinguishing feature to differentiate people who lived cheek by jowl and in other respects had similar lifestyles. As we shall shortly see, this bigotry was not confined to just one religion. She worked in a cotton mill within walking distance of her home until she married my father on 5 August, 1935 when she was 21.

Herbert Maher was one year older than my mother. His family and hers were neighbours. They lived within a few streets of each other. The families knew each other. But the Maher family was Catholic. My father was the fifth child of a family which grew to eight; as my mother had six siblings, it would seem that large families were not, as is popularly

1

believed, a monopoly of Catholics. When the wedding of Herbert Maher and Lilian Redman was announced, the marriage of a Catholic to a Protestant, in a Catholic church, with the usual mandatory undertaking that any children would be brought up in the Catholic faith and would go to Catholic schools, the members of my mother's family were forbidden to attend; or to have anything further to do with her. It was to be many years before they spoke again. Shortly before my mother's death, the boot was to be on the other foot. My father's youngest brother married a Protestant girl. Another mixed marriage. But this time it was a Church of England wedding. Catholics would never enter a Protestant church and the Maher family was ordered not to attend. My mother, but, cruelly, not my father, was the only one to offer support; she had suffered mightily on her own account. The wedding photograph on which she appears is the one photograph of her which I still have.

This bigotry from both sides of the religious divide was to have severe consequences. I have little doubt that my mother's health was not helped by an estrangement which continued until shortly before her death. And my father's brother, John, was never fully reconciled to his large, but now hostile, family for the rest of his life. The misery which was created by this extreme intolerance and the brutal and hard-hearted manner in which people at their most vulnerable were cast out of their families was heart-breaking. And this from those who professed a shared belief in God. It was as if they had little else to look forward to in life other than solidarity with their co-religionists and unthinking enmity to the other side. The narcissism of small differences.

The Maher family was split between strong women and weak men. My father was one of the weak men. He worked in the newspaper industry as a printer's assistant. The actual elements of the job consisted simply of tying up parcels of newspapers with string before they were put into vans for delivery to newspaper wholesalers and distributors. It was simple, undemanding work, but, because the work was controlled by NATSOPA, the notoriously militant printing trades union, it paid relatively well. Although its members might be working at the *Daily Express*, the *News of the World*, or the *Manchester Evening News*, the effective employer was the union, and it paid out the wages at the end of the week. It would determine which workmen were to be directed to which newspaper each day, and was ferocious in protecting the interests of its members, who usually had a job for life. As well as being undemanding, the nature of the work meant that there was a fair amount of idle time in between printing runs. That was when any self-respecting NATSOPA member would be found in the pub. And my father was usually at the head of the pack. Despite strict licensing laws, it was always possible to obtain alcoholic drink throughout the night and my father was rarely entirely sober. But he was not alone in that. It was almost a badge of honour in the legendary drinking culture of the newspaper industry.

When my parents married, their first and, as it turned out, only home, was at 94 Viaduct Street in Beswick. The districts of Ancoats, Beswick, Ardwick, Miles Platting and Collyhurst were huddled together around the eastern edge of the Manchester city centre. There was little to choose between them, although the residents of Beswick always thought that they were a cut above those from Ancoats, and very much better than the Collyhurst lot. Yet another example of the narcissism of small differences. They were populated by row upon row of identical two up and two down terraced houses built in the nineteenth century for the teeming workers of the surrounding mills and engineering and chemical factories. In the slum clearance housing revolution, which started modestly in the 1930s and accelerated rapidly in the 1950s and 1960s, the whole of this area was demolished and most of its residents moved to the massive new housing estates within the extended outer-city boundaries to the south and east of Manchester. This honoured the wartime pledge to build 'homes for heroes,' and fulfilled Harold Macmillan's promise, when he was Housing Minister, to build 300,000 houses a year. Today, in a good year, we build little more than 120,000.

Viaduct Street ran from Ashton New Road (the New Road) – where Manchester City's new football stadium is now situated – to Ashton Old Road (the Old Road), and was immediately opposite the railway line from which it was separated by a brick wall which must have been about six feet in height. Number 94 was, in most respects, the same as its neighbours. It was brick built and the front door opened directly onto the street. A rare opportunity for the house-proud to show an expression of some individuality was presented by the doorstep and its immediate surrounds. 'Donkey' stones had been used for generations in the working class areas of the North of England to scrub and colour the step in various shades of cream and brown; and housewives on their hands and knees had an ideal occasion to gossip with their neighbours. Once over the step, the door opened directly into the gas-lit front room. It had a coal fire, with its black-leaded grate. The front room led to the kitchen. Here there was a pot earthenware sink with running cold water, a gas stove, and a door leading to a small enclosed yard and the lavatory. On laundry days, you would hear the background noise of the creaking mangle, as it squeezed the moisture out of the washing, before it was pegged out on the clothes line to dry. A gate from the yard led to a narrow entry, which separated the parallel rows of houses, and it was through the gate that the dustbin was collected and the coal delivered. A wooden staircase went from the kitchen to the two small bedrooms, where candles would provide illumination.

I was born on 5 December 1935. My earliest memories are mainly about the war, which was to start almost four years later. My father was called up to join the army, but he was not to see active service, or ever to leave the country, on account of my mother's health which was already poor. Towards the end of the war he had several spells of leave at home on compassionate grounds as her health deteriorated further. My first awareness of the war was as a result of the need for blackout curtains and blinds to ensure that no light should leak out into the street and be visible to overhead enemy planes. This blackout was enforced rigorously by the air-raid wardens who would hammer on the front-door should any trace of light be seen. During air raids we would shelter under the stairs of our next door neighbour, six of us huddled together (I had a brother by then) until the all-clear siren sounded. For some reason, the stair-well in our own house had been boarded up. Later, there was a newly built brick air-raid shelter, round the corner in Devon Street, where we would congregate after the air-raid warning siren and sing songs. The refrain that sticks in my mind is the one which begins: 'Ten green bottles hanging on the wall.' Those who were fortunate enough to have a garden had their own individual Anderson shelters, but I was not aware of this at the time. In any event, I think I would have preferred our own, communal, sing-a-long arrangement.

The morning after one German bombing expedition, in the blitz of 1940 (I would have been five), I walked towards a corner shop just a street away. But the shop was no longer there, and the street corner was now a bomb site. Scattered around were dented cans of dried egg and tinned bacon and large fragments of shrapnel, which were a particular prize. A number of people several blocks away from ours were killed in one heavy bombing raid and, on another occasion, a nearby unexploded bomb caused a scare until it was defused; but our little family reached the end of the war unscathed. VE Day in 1945 was celebrated at street parties with union jacks and bunting, tea and cakes, and dancing in the street; a typically modest British recognition of such a momentous event. The signs of war did not entirely disappear as US servicemen were still stationed in Britain, many of them in nearby Burtonwood. Their troop trains would sometimes travel along the railway line opposite our house and several of us would sit on the railway wall calling out to them as the train slowed on its approach to its terminus in Manchester. We were rewarded, on one never to be forgotten occasion, with a flurry of packets of chewing gum being thrown to us from the carriage windows.

When I was five I started at Birley Street School, which was two streets behind Viaduct Street. Birley Street was not a Catholic school. I can only imagine that the distraction of war, and perhaps my father's absence in the army, meant that there had not been the usual religious pressures. It was certainly a more convenient arrangement as the nearest Catholic school was a 20-minute walk away and involved crossing the New Road. The only memory I have of Birley

Street is from a fall when running home at the end of the school day. I had been taught, by my mother, french knitting and was carrying the cotton reel and wool in my hand. Rather than the usual crotcheting needle, I had a large darning needle. It broke on impact and pierced the palm of my hand. I remember that I cried a lot.

Convenient or not, within a year I was transferred to St. Anne's Catholic school in Ancoats. The religious imperative had been re-established. My new routine then involved the daily walk, crossing the busy main road, to and from my new school, usually alone, later with my younger brother (although he soon developed his own independence), and occasionally with one of the teachers who lived nearby and who always sought to offer me gentle encouragement. A new treat was my first pair of wooden clogs, and as I ran along I could kick sparks from the hard contact of the metal runners with the cobbled street. The headmaster was Mr. Clancy who had a reputation as a disciplinarian, and who wielded the cane with enthusiasm. I later came to know his two sons from whom I learned that their father had been an important figure in the Irish nationalist movement. He certainly had a difficult job at St. Anne's. It was the largest Catholic boy's school within the Salford diocese, and these were all boys from poor homes. But he had gathered together a talented group of teachers and I cannot remember an unhappy school-day whilst I was at St. Anne's. In retrospect, it is clear that they saw me as a promising pupil and had ambitions for me to gain a scholarship to one of the city's two Catholic grammar schools; which might have been a first for a St. Anne's boy. At the time, it meant little to me, and they were much keener on the idea than I was. At dinner time – in the middle of the school day – some boys would eat their sandwiches, some would eat at home, and some would buy chips from the nearby chip shop – I never remember fish being on the menu. I would sometimes have chips, and on other occasions a sandwich in the home of a schoolboy who lived close to the school. Viaduct Street was too far away. Afterwards, many of us would congregate at the local 'cut'. This was an evil smelling, stagnant backwater of the Ashton Canal, littered with floating debris. St. Anne's Catholic schoolboys would line up on one side of the 'cut' and the Protestant boys of a rival school lined up on the other side. They then proceeded to chuck stones at each other until it was time for afternoon lessons.

More than seventy years later, on a visit to the Tate Gallery, I was to see the same streets of terraced houses, the same school, the hospital which I had visited after a fall in St. Anne's school-yard, and the fairground I had visited at Easter-time. It was the Lowry exhibition. I could feel and almost smell the mood and atmosphere and acrid smoke from the train engines going by Viaduct Street. In his painting of Ancoats Hospital Outpatients' Hall, I could well have been sitting there clutching my knee. And in his depiction of the Silcock Brothers circus on a Good Friday at Daisy Nook, I could easily have been one of his stick figures wandering around the fairground. One of Lowry's children. During the war Lowry worked as a fire-watcher on top of one of the city centre department stores watching for incendiary bombs. Between 1910 and 1952, he worked for the Pall Mall Property Company in those same working class areas of Manchester in which I was born. He could have been the rent man who knocked on our door each Monday morning to collect his dues. A full rent book, with each week's rent carefully entered, and with no arrears, was a prize to be savoured, and was a prerequisite when seeking any other desirable tenancy.

Now, L. S. Lowry is a Manchester hero. The River Irwell, another former evil smelling waterway of central Manchester, has been gentrified into the Venice of the North, and boasts both a Lowry hotel and a Lowry museum. And that bleak part of Manchester, which Lowry painted, and in which I lived, has also been transformed. After the evacuation of most of its indigenous population, it had become an industrial wasteland. But, with the building of a stadium and other facilities for the Commonwealth Games, and then its further development by Manchester City Football Club, it has now become one of the major sports centres in the country, surrounded by trees and wild-flower meadows. And there is a New Viaduct Street. I wonder what Lowry would make of it all.

I left the Tate Gallery with a spring in my step, and felt a further gentle push towards writing this memoir.

As well as the rent man, there were other regular visitors, some more welcome than others. There was the friendly clatter and chatter of the dustbin men in the back entry; the rag and bone man with his horse and cart travelling through the streets with his traditional cry of 'Any old iron?' He would take almost anything – old clothes (often literally rags), kettles and pans, bits of broken furniture. Whatever could be found. In return he would offer the 'Donkey' stones used for buffing-up the doorsteps. These stones were never bought from shops; they always came from the rag and bone man. It was said that they were called 'Donkey' stones because of the donkey leading the cart. Another horse and cart visitor sold sarsaparilla and dandelion and burdock from heavy earthenware jugs. Although these refreshing drinks were sold door-to-door, milk had to be collected from Curley's dairy on the New Road, also in jugs. A daily visitor was the street dawn patrol of the 'knocker-up.' He was paid pennies a week by each household so that, with his long stick, he would rattle the bedroom window from the street, at an agreed hour, to ensure that the bread-winner got to the local factory or cotton mill on time. The more frugal and canny would rely on the rattle at the next door window and save their pennies. Alarm clocks were still a long way off. What I never found out was who knocked up the knocker-up.

A less welcome visitor was the tally man. He would usually call on Friday, pay day. Before the days of hire purchase and credit cards, he was the only source of credit for working class people. A borrower would receive a voucher, a form of cheque, for (say) five pounds, which could be used to buy clothing and household goods at designated local shops. This would be repaid, with interest, over 20 weeks at several shillings each week. Neighbours kept a sharp eye on the houses at which the tally man called. And they could become quite agitated if the knock on the door elicited no response. My grandmother was always adamant on the subject of the tally man – 'we never buy on tick.'

My brother Alan was born on 12 August 1937, 20 months after me. That was to complete the family. As we grew up together, it soon became clear that he was more suited than I was to the rough and tumble of street life in Ancoats and Beswick. He was the tough one, and was not afraid to use his fists. I was more reserved, shy I suppose, and perhaps a bit of a coward. He was much the more popular. Years later, when I went to a St. Anne's re-union for a television programme, nobody knew me. They all thought I was Alan.

I must have had my first money-box when I was about five or six. The box was in the shape of a book with a slot for coins. It was provided by the Midland Bank, and they were the sole holders of the key which could open it up. A coin would always be placed in my hand, for the money-box, whenever I saw any of my several uncles. Whether this was an exclusively working-class practice I do not know, but it is a tradition which, sadly, no longer seems to exist. When it began to feel heavy, I would take the 'book' along to the bank's impressive premises at the end of the New Road, just by the library. I suppose in the early days I would be with my mother. On arrival, a bank clerk would unlock the box, and the proceeds would be placed in a savings account which had been opened in my name.

An important date in the Catholic calendar in Manchester and Salford was the annual Whit walks. Children from all the Catholic schools in the diocese walked in procession from their respective schools to congregate together in the city centre. It was an occasion when most parents wanted their children to look their best. Suits were bought which, were it not for the pressure of the Whit walks, might not otherwise have been purchased. It was a boon for the tally man. My mother dressed Alan and me identically – as if we were twins. One of her last excursions with us was to 'Burton the Tailor' on the New Road where we were both measured for navy blue, double-breasted, serge suits, ready for the Walks. Proper suits for two boys aged nine and 11 – and our first with long trousers.

It is remarkable that poor people were able to wear well-tailored, made-to-measure suits (although not without some sacrifice) when today it is thought to be the prerogative of the rich. The mass-produced ready-made alterna-

11

tive did not then exist. My mother would prepare us for Mass on Sunday with our 'best' (only) suit, shirt and tie and well-polished shoes. As soon as we left the house Alan would tear the tie from his neck, thrust it into his trouser pocket, and almost deliberately scuff his shoes. (It is only as I write this that I realise that our youngest son, Jeremy, at the same age, had a similar behaviour pattern). I kept my tie in place and my shoes remained highly polished. A regular goody two-shoes! As children we were not close, and, as an adult, Alan became a Jehovah's Witness. This meant that he could no longer have any relationship with those who did not share his beliefs. So the divorce was now total. Religious extremism again. It is a pity.

My father, until after my mother's death, was a somewhat shadowy figure whom I rarely saw. First, he was in the army, and then he was working at night on the newspapers. I do not believe that he always treated my mother well. On nights when he was not working he would return late from the pub and Alan and I, from our bedroom, would hear raised voices. I suspect that there might also have been raised hands. On a more cheerful occasion, I remember that he came into the house towards the end of the war for a weekend's compassionate leave. He had a kit-back over his shoulder. Inside were two really large rabbits. A hutch was soon knocked together and placed in the back yard. That was to be their new home. Several weeks later, on an early morning visit with food and drink, I found that we now had some baby rabbits. But they did not survive. And, shortly afterwards, neither did their parents. It must have been very cold in that backyard.

The mother I remember was never in good health. But she brought up her two boys whilst often alone, and, when not alone, without any other practical help. And the two boys were always impeccably turned out. She also contributed to the family budget, before she became too ill, by doing weekend work as a waitress at the Mitchell Arms on the New Road. She suffered from a disease of the kidneys which today could probably be treated successfully, but at that time was usually a death warrant. She would lose energy quickly, would take to her bed, and then might be a little better the next day. But there was a gradual, cumulative deterioration that turned out to be irreversible.

I have no recollection of any books in the house, but I do remember the comics. The *Dandy* and the *Beano* were alright with their cartoon strips, but I much preferred the *Adventure*, the *Champion* and the *Rover*, which had proper stories and real heroes, about whose escapades I would read each week. The comics were brought home by my father. They were published by the wealthy Scottish family of D. C. Thompson, who shared distribution arrangements with the newspapers on which my father worked. He was later to provide the same service for his grandchildren, calling each Friday with a bunch of comics tucked under his arm.

When my father was working, there would also be a newspaper. It would usually be the *Daily Express* with the *News of the World* on Sundays, but in later years it was the *Manchester Guardian*. Other news came from the wireless. Its energy source was an accumulator; a heavy, clumsy contraption which had to be taken for regular re-charging to a local shop. My mother encouraged me to read the newspapers, and, as the war raged throughout Europe, I used to follow the battle plans, which they reproduced daily, with diagrams showing tanks and arrows and front lines. She also encouraged me to write letters to my Auntie Betty.

13

She would always read them before they were posted, and one of my few scraps of memory suggests that she could be quite pedantic. I had written that my father had now left the army and had got his demob suit. 'Demobilisation, is the proper word,' she said, 'not demob.'

Auntie Betty was my father's sister, a little older than him, and was my godmother. But she was now Sister Mary of St Cuthberga, a nun in a convent. She belonged to a closed order and I have no recollection of seeing her until in my adult life, when the changes in the Vatican enabled her to travel. Betty was considered by all who knew her to be the most saintly of people. She wrote intelligent, loving letters to me and said that I must look after my mother. When, many years later, I did eventually meet her I was able to see for myself what a compassionate and caring person she was. But she had an innocence about her and a manner and way of talking which reflected her background. She once told me about somebody she had recently met. 'He is a Protestant,' she said, 'but he is not a bad man.' She had not the slightest idea as to how offensive that might sound.

Amongst the other boys around Viaduct Street, I had established a reputation as being good at reading and spelling. I am not sure on what evidence, but perhaps the bar was not set at a particularly high level. In any event, at a time when I was perhaps no more than six years of age I remember being marched round by some of the bigger boys to a corner shop to read out the legend on the legion of products in the shop window – like some kind of circus freak. The name Phensic still stays in my mind.

The highlight of the week was the Saturday afternoon matinee at the Mosely picture house where a Roy Rogers film with his loyal horse Trigger was often the main event. On my return home, usually with Alan, the treat would continue with a hot dinner usually involving roast beef, roast potatoes and a thick brown gravy. Heaven! I must have watched more than cowboy films because, mystifyingly, I wrote to the film studios, asking, successfully, for autographed photographs of Olivia de Havilland, Sonja Henie and Jean Kent.

The other source of entertainment was the wireless and on a Saturday night we would often sit together listening to the currently popular singers, with my favourite being Anne Shelton, whilst my mother and Alan favoured Vera Lynn. An unusual change of scenery involved a rare excursion across the Old Road, at the other end of Viaduct Street, to the Ardwick Hippodrome, which was in Ardwick Green. It was January 1947, and Alan and I had gone there together to see our first pantomime, *Aladdin*. We walked back, quite late, on a particularly cold and dark night. One cannot imagine it being allowed to happen today.

That particular winter of 1947 was the coldest anyone could remember. For those who were still weary from the war, it was to pose a further test of stamina and character. Many did not survive; and it was to prove too much for my mother. The snow fell in January, and it did not clear until the end of March. The freeze was exacerbated by transport difficulties and industrial disputes. Coal deliveries could not get through and there were power cuts. When the thaw did arrive there were new problems. The thick layer of snow on the roofs had provided a comforting layer of insulation against the extremes of wind and cold. Now, the melting snow found newly established cracks between the slates and the roofing timbers. At the initial breakthrough, torrents of water cascaded into the bedrooms. This developed into a steady, hypnotic, drip, drip, drip. Buckets and every available

15

pot and pan were brought into duty to collect the water as it fell from the ceiling. It was to be several weeks before the overworked landlord's men could carry out the repairs.

As my mother's health deteriorated, she was no longer able to go to the shops, and soon, she was also no longer able to cook. She was increasingly confined to her bed and, as the upstairs was virtually uninhabitable, the bed was now brought down into the front room. The household shopping duties were delegated to me, and I also assumed a modest cooking role. I would prepare a list, dictated by my mother, and do the rounds of the shops. The butcher, grocer, baker, and dairy – and also the Co-op with the all-important 'divi' number, to ensure that the purchases qualified for the annual dividend. I was soon a familiar figure, and was known to have a keen awareness of the prices. The cooking consisted of preparing what was described as a nourishing soup. I would put suitable bones, selected for this purpose by the butcher, into a pan of boiling water, and then add seasoning, carrots, turnips and other vegetables, whilst it gently simmered on the stove. I would then carefully skim the scum, which gathered with some persistence, from the surface foam of the developing soup.

The last errand I ran from Viaduct Street was at the request of the doctor. It was to the chemist on the New Road for glycerine, which was to be used to moisten my mother's lips. I was then spending my nights at my grandmother's home in Clayton. The following day I was told by my Auntie Kathleen that my mother had died. Kathleen later told me that her final words had been to ask 'Who will look after my boys?' It was May 1947. My father was distraught and never fully recovered. He was rarely ever again to mention my mother's name, other than in despair, when more than usually drunk. It was just too much for him. My mother was 33 when she died; my father was 34, I was 11 and Alan was nine.

II
AN UNUSUAL CHILDHOOD

There seemed no opportunity to grieve my mother's death. The enormity of the loss was not felt by an 11-year-old boy. It was only with the passing of the years that my appreciation of its full significance developed. To realise what she has missed and what I have missed. She never met Barbara, my wife, or her three grandchildren; was totally unaware of my business exploits; never saw our lovely home in the country; never visited London or ever went to a foreign country. And I lost a mother whom I hardly knew.

But, at the time, life just moved on. The temporary move to my grandmother's home in Seymour Road South became a permanent one. It was in Clayton which was a 15 minute bus ride from Viaduct Street. The trolley buses, numbers 26 and 27, started in Stephenson Square and went along the New Road, travelling east towards Ashton-under-Lyne and Stalybridge. My grandparents had moved to Seymour Road from Palmerston Street, which was a close neighbour of Viaduct Street.

Palmerston Street was to be the unlikely focus of conversation at a reception at 10 Downing Street many years later. At the reception, I fell into discussion with Professor Roland Smith. 'The professor,' as he was usually known, was chairman of House of Fraser, which then owned Harrods, and he was defending the company from attack by Tiny Rowland's Lonrho. 'Keep your tanks off my lawn,' he had famously warned Rowland. 'The professor' had a mixed reputation, being thought in the City to be more an academic than a businessman, and in academia as being more a businessman than an academic. Bernard Levin had once pricked his academic pretensions in one of his more acerbic and trenchant polemics for *The Times*. 'The chairman of House of Fraser,' Levin wrote, 'is a professor. A professor of marketing. A professor of marketing at UMIST' (which Levin thought not to be a proper university), and, the final put-down: 'The Joe Hyman professor of marketing.' Bernard Levin did not see marketing as a suitable subject for academia. He would be even less happy if he were alive today and could see even newer universities offering degree courses in sports psychology and gender studies.

Roland Smith was a fellow Mancunian who had retained his Manchester accent. We had not met before. I asked him from which part of Manchester he came and he said that he was born in Beswick. 'Which street?' I asked. 'Palmerston Street,' he replied. So here we were, two poor boys from Manchester, born in neighbouring, grubby streets, meeting for the first time in the home of the prime minister. I later came to know Roland well and he was to confide in me about his state of paranoia at the attentions of Tiny Rowland. The last time I saw him was when he called at our flat in Regent's Park, having been asked by a mutual friend to warn me of the risks involved in publishing my business memoir. He had become a bit of a conspiracy theorist.

The house in Seymour Road, number 88, had a crucial extra bedroom and a musty front parlour; this was meant to be used on special occasions, but these did not seem to come along with any great frequency. The front door opened onto a tiny garden, no more than six feet deep, which was rarely tended, and with the only hint of green being from a rather dusty shrub. Beyond the back yard, however, was a field which, in the war, had been used as a base for barrage balloons and for an anti-aircraft battery. It now provided a welcome open aspect, although surrounded on all sides by other rows of identical terraced houses. The kitchen was large enough to accommodate a clothes maiden, which meant that washing could be hung inside the house rather than on an outside line; for those living in the house, it cannot have been the healthiest way to dry the laundry. Another feature was a tin bath, which was brought into use for Friday night ablutions. The kitchen was also home to legions of beetles, with hard shiny-backed cases, and which, when the light was switched on (we had electricity), would scuttle across the stone floor back into their hiding holes, in the cracks at the bottom of the walls. The front bedroom was occupied by my grandparents and the middle bedroom was to be for my father, Alan and me. Auntie Kathleen was the one remaining sibling of my father's still at home, and she had the back bedroom. Fortunately, Uncle John had recently left home and married, otherwise things would not have worked out quite so easily. He was later to re-appear at 94 Viaduct Street.

Both my paternal grandparents were born in Manchester, of Irish parents. My grandmother's maiden name was Connelly. The Mahers were poor Irish Catholics and would hope to have been described as members of the 'respectable working classes'. Their legions populated large swathes of the North of England. There was a certain amount of prejudice. The stories of lodging houses with notices stating 'no Irish or dogs', (this was before the influx of West Indian immigrants, after which 'blacks' were added to the proscribed list) and job advertisements stipulating that 'Catholics need not apply' were not apocryphal. Maher, along with its alternative form Meagher (both pronounced

'Maar'), derives from the Irish name O'Meachair, meaning 'son of the generous host'. The chief seat of the O'Maher clan was near Devil Bit's Mountain, outside of Roscrea, in County Tipperary. The old family motto is reported to be 'Deus protector noster' – God is our protector.

Today, I am occasionally reminded of those sectarian times by a member of my tennis group. He is an unbending Ulsterman of decidedly firm views, with whom I have formed an unlikely friendship. When hearing an Irish sounding name, I once said to him: 'When we hear the name Hugh we know, don't we, whether it is a Catholic name or a Protestant name?' 'Terry,' he responded, looking at me very directly, 'I don't need to hear the name, just show me the face.'

My grandmother was a most remarkable woman. She had brought up eight children; six had married, one was in a convent, and one was still at home. Now she was to take on the responsibility – for a while at least – of another family. Grandfather had worked for the 'corporation' in what is now called refuse collection; first as the driver of a horse-drawn cart, and later of a motor vehicle. He was a carter. His father had been a carter and his two eldest sons became carters. Carters or not, they would always be turned out on Sunday mornings, for Mass and the pub afterwards, in three-piece suits, a collared shirt, and a tie.

My grandfather's mother was illiterate and had signed his birth certificate with the traditional illiterate's sign of a X. In the First World War he was exposed to mustard gas and was no longer in good health. He now worked as a gate-keeper for a local manufacturer. On my way home from school, I would sometimes see him resting on a low garden wall recovering his breath at the end of his day's work. Although he was always in work, as were his children, the family income was, inevitably, modest, and was supplemented in the early years by my grandmother's work on a stall in a city centre market. But they did not have a bad life. In between the wars, her large family spent the wakes week holiday in the Isle of Man – not the down-market, vulgar Blackpool where the neighbours went. There was always food on the table and they were all respectably dressed.

The Sundays I first experienced at Seymour Road were an absolute treat. Mass at the local St Willibrord's church was mandatory. But then things looked up. The hot breakfast boasted fried eggs, bacon and - my special - melted cheese. I would then scan the newspaper, and perhaps listen to family favourites on the wireless, whilst my grandparents took their weekly walk to a nearby pub where they met friends. My grandmother would order half a pint of mild beer and my grandfather a pint of bitter. They might repeat the order. But that would be their limit. At one time they might have visited public houses more frequently and perhaps imbibed more freely; but that was now the extent of their routine. And alcohol was rarely to be found in the house; if you wanted a drink you went to the pub. At lunch (or dinner as it was then called) there would be roast beef and all the trimmings; and at tea time, around six o'clock, it was boiled ham and 'best butter' – not the scorned margarine which graced the table at week-days – spread on thick slices of still-wartime off-white bread.

Grandmother (her children called her Sarah Jane when out of her hearing) had her own tailor who would attend to take measurements at her home. I was present when she took delivery of a rather splendid overcoat. 'This will see me out,' she said cheerfully. Her pessimism, thank God, was not justified, as she was to live for another 20 years. It is difficult to understand how she was able to achieve so much. Quite apart from the financial issues, rationing did not end until 1954 and government issued coupons were required to purchase food and clothing. She was fiercely independent, never borrowed money, and never accepted charity, whether it was from the state or any other agency. She was in total charge of the family finances, and household bills were paid from an enormous purse which was strapped round her waist underneath her skirt.

My new route to St. Anne's School involved a ride on the trolley bus which I caught on the New Road, at the end of Seymour Road, and which took me from Clayton back to Ancoats. The journey was a little more than half an hour door-to-door. I had been back at school for several weeks after my mother's funeral when the teacher who had occasionally walked with me from Viaduct Street asked if I had heard the result of the scholarship examination which I had taken earlier in the year. He looked concerned at my lack of news, and at my lunch break (dinner time) I retraced my steps to 94 Viaduct Street. My Uncle John and his newish wife had already taken over the tenancy of our old house. She greeted me warmly at the door and there on the mantelpiece, over the fireplace, was a letter addressed to me. I had been accepted to go to the Xaverian College.

Before starting my new school, I had to endure the summer holidays. Start of term at Xaverian College was much later than at St. Anne's and the other secondary schools. The weeks seemed interminable. I had an offer to spend one of the weeks at the home of my Auntie Nelly, who lived in Stockport. She was my mother's half -sister; after the death of her first husband, my maternal grandmother had re-married, and my mother was the first child of the second marriage. I took with me a very young, hardly house-trained puppy. It must have been given to me to offer some kind of comfort, although, at the time, I had never shown any interest in dogs. In any event, I set off, alone, still only eleven years of age, to visit my Auntie Nelly, with the dog, in a carrier- bag, clutched closely to my chest. I boarded the trolley bus at the New Road, walked from Stevenson Square to Piccadilly bus station, and found a bus to take me to Mersey Square in Stockport. Once there, I took a third bus to a housing estate in Adswood, and then, asking passers-by for help along the way, I found the house where my Auntie Nelly lived with her two sons. I had not been there before, and had only previously seen Auntie Nelly at my maternal grandmother's home, which was also in Clayton, not too far from Seymour Road. I rang the doorbell, and she opened the door, but looked aghast when she saw the puppy. 'You can't bring that dog in,' she said, 'I've got a cat.' She told me that I must return to Seymour Road, leave the puppy there, and then I would be very welcome. Without having crossed the threshold, I retraced my steps. Three buses back home, and then three more buses back again to Adswood. It must have been a journey of at least two hours each way; more than six hours in all. And I cannot remember any refreshment. It had been a dispiriting day.

I did not feel very welcome at my Auntie Nelly's. I overheard one of my two cousins - they were both much older than me - ask his mother when I was leaving. I was glad to return home – three more buses – at the end of the week. I have no recollection of what happened to the puppy. I assume that it was returned to its original owner, or that some other new home was found for it; it had not proved to be a practical idea for an 11-year-old boy with little other support.

Xaverian College was one of only two Catholic grammar schools for boys in Manchester. The other was St. Bede's College, which had a reputation as a seminary, preparing a number of its pupils for the priesthood. Xaverian was founded in 1872, and, since 1903, had been situated in Victoria Park which was to the south and west of Manchester – a 15-minute bus ride from the city centre. It was gated parkland in which were a number of substantial properties originally built as homes for Manchester's wealthy mill and factory owners. In another of life's coincidences, Lowry had at one time lived in Victoria Park and went to his first school there. By the 1950s, however, it was already looking a little down-at-heel, although this description certainly did not apply to the Xaverian College. The school buildings were impressive, certainly to this impressionable new boy, had been extended in recent years, and surrounded a cricket pitch with its own pavilion and a large open assembly area and playground. Xaverian had high academic standards but did not have quite the distinction of its near neighbour the non-Catholic Manchester Grammar School. It was a definite step-up from St. Anne's Ancoats. Sadly, since 1977, it has been a sixth form college, having been a victim, with many, many others, of the educational vandalism of Anthony Crosland and Shirley Williams.

Most of the teachers belonged to the order of St. Francis Xavier and they were led by a noted, stern disciplinarian, Brother Martin. It seemed that I had swapped one disciplinarian, Mr. Clancy at St. Anne's, for another. Brother Martin was an unbending man and Christian charity was a concept with which he did not seem to be familiar.

25

He always seemed, at least to this small boy, to be angry. However, I caught him towards the end of his tenure, and perhaps he had been kinder when he was younger. But I doubt it. Many years later, I met one of my literary heroes, Anthony Burgess. I said to him that we both came from the same mean streets of Manchester, but that my streets were meaner than his. I mentioned Xaverian College, where he had also been a pupil. 'Ah,' he exclaimed, 'Brother Martin!'

Xaverian provided a traditional, Jesuitical education and the school was a member of the Headmasters' Conference, which meant that, technically, it was a public school. It had a small number of boarders, and around 10 per cent of its intake, (a government requirement), were non-Catholics. In the first term at my new school I settled in surprisingly quickly. The daily journey, with a change of buses, took about one hour each way, but that was manageable. I took the trolley bus to Grey Mare Lane, and then a more conventional petrol-driven bus, the number 53, to Victoria Park. The teachers were firm but encouraging, and the form-master and maths teacher, Brother Cyril – who was the newest and youngest member of staff – had taken me under his wing. The homework was not onerous. At the end-of-term examinations, I was placed third in my form, doing well in maths, English, and Latin. Brother Cyril took me to one side to say that the two boys ahead of me were not from the new intake and therefore had an unfair advantage. Brother Martin's comment at the end of my first report was just two words – 'Well done.' I was not to do so well at school again.

In the late spring – it would have been close to the first anniversary of my mother's death – I was unwell with a high temperature and a persistent cough which had outlived an earlier cold. I was unable to go to school, and the doctor was called. As soon as he saw the tell-tale red blotches on my legs he diagnosed tuberculosis. TB was endemic in the deprived areas of the major industrial cities and was highly contagious. I was sharing a bed in a small room with my brother and my father (he would usually join us after his night-shift in the early hours of the morning). The doctor immediately arranged for my admission to hospital, and the following day I was in an ambulance on a three hour journey to Abergele Sanatorium in North Wales. It was to be almost another year before I returned home.

An X-ray examination disclosed what was described as a 'shadow' on my left lung. In the context of the disease as a whole, this was relatively minor and at an early stage. The drugs, which in just a few years' time were to be used so successfully in the treatment of tuberculosis (and with which later I was to become very familiar), had not then been fully developed, and the only 'cure' was fresh air and rest. Beds were pushed outside onto the veranda in all weathers, and the patients exposed to the elements. This of course did not always work and many did not survive. My own condition cannot ever have been really serious. I apparently made steady progress and cannot remember feeling properly ill at any time. However, the medical establishment, quite understandably, were extremely cautious in their assessment of a potentially 'killer' disease, and would not want to release me until they were totally re-assured.

Abergele was a children's hospital and there was a desultory attempt at some kind of teaching but it was more in the nature of occupational therapy. The patients were too disparate in age and ability levels, and also in health, for any kind of effective academic teaching. When I left Abergele

27

to return to the Xaverian College, I would have a lot of ground to make up. Most of the patients were from the Manchester area and each Sunday a coach left the city centre to take visitors to the hospital. My grandmother came to see me several times, as did my father, but it was difficult for them to visit on a regular basis; my father because of his work (the Saturday night shift was the best paid), and my grandmother because of her advancing years and her other family commitments. Most Sundays I was without visitors and it was then the fact that the family was no longer complete was most forcibly brought home to me. I missed my mother. As Christmas approached, there was a welcome diversion. The hard pressed sole member of the teaching staff organised several of us in producing a short sketch based on Christopher Robin which we presented to visiting parents. Soon into the New Year, I was told that I could return home to Manchester, but before I could resume my interrupted studies at the Xaverian College, there was to be further disruption.

The fact that I now had a history of tuberculosis meant that the family was placed at the top of the waiting list for a new council house. My father decided that we (he, my brother and I) would leave Seymour Road and live together in the flat which had been allocated to us in Woodhouse Park. It was not to be a success. Woodhouse Park was 10 miles from Manchester city centre and on the southernmost fringe of the sprawling estates of Wythenshawe, the area which, at that time, housed most of those displaced from the town centre. It bordered on Cheshire, which was the gateway to another world, and was close to Ringway Airport (now called Manchester International). As soon as I returned to my grandmother's house, we moved out to Woodhouse Park. We were the first tenants of the two bedroomed, newly built flat and we had only a few sticks of basic furniture. There were bare, recently plastered walls; large, only sparsely curtained, windows; and uncarpeted, concrete floors. It was cold. Very cold! Colder even than Viaduct Street in the big freeze of two years before. And it cannot have been very healthy.

By default, the responsibility for shopping, cooking, and generally looking after the flat fell to me. My father soon lost heart. It was a long journey to and from his work, he had no friends or friendly pubs locally, and he did not always return home. Woodhouse Park was such a soulless, only half-completed estate. Just endless rows of new flats and houses; no shops, no pubs, no atmosphere, empty streets, and certainly no park. It was in total contrast to the friendly, over-neighbourly, busy streets of Beswick, with a pub or a shop on every corner. Woodhouse Park was a ghost town; a desert without an oasis. A nightmare. We stuck it out for a little more than a year before giving up and going back to Seymour Road.

Whilst all this was going on, I was trying to re-establish myself at school. I had missed two and a half terms. On my return, Brother Cyril, who was no longer my form-master, sought me out to say that I would need to do extra homework to catch up but that he was sure that I could manage it. He introduced me to Brother Stephen, my new form-master who also took Latin, and explained to him that I had done well in my first term. A programme of work was quickly established. But I soon fell behind. One morning, in front of the whole class, Brother Stephen held up a piece of homework which I had submitted. He said that it was a disgrace. And he was right. It was a Latin exercise which I had set out on a tea-stained shabby sheet of paper. It is clear to me now that it would be a mistake to use the excuse of a difficult home life to justify such an embarrassing episode, and also the subsequent further disappointments at school. The home environment was by no means the whole story. The fact is that I had been used to excelling at school-work and was not used to being behind, or to receiving criticism. I did not respond well – I was far too thin-skinned – and there were to be no more pats on the back. I was not sufficiently determined and, as I fell further behind, I was too easily discouraged and lost enthusiasm; not surprisingly, my teachers lost interest. I was entered for only five 'O' levels and passed in just four. The high hopes of Brother Cyril (who was later to succeed Brother Martin as headmaster) were dashed; and I had squandered the chance of a first class education. I never realised at the time quite what an opportunity it was that I had missed. I was 16 when I left the Xaverian College to look for work.

My father never seemed a happy man. This was particularly so after my mother's death. He was a little over six feet in height – or so he claimed – which was tall by the standards of those times. He was slimly built, with dark, centrally parted hair, and spectacles which he took to wearing when he no longer had any alternative. He was always dressed, whether for work or the pub, in a smart suit (but not the three-piece version favoured by his father and older brothers), shirt and tie. And he possessed a prized Crombie overcoat. He was a little vain (an accusation which might also have been levelled at his elder son). He had little to look forward to apart from the pub. And, as he was in the habit of upsetting people, he had to change pubs on a fairly regular basis.

Fortunately, in Beswick and Ancoats, and around the Manchester newspaper offices, there was an abundance of welcoming public houses. His preferred brew was Chester's bitter, which was reputedly the strongest of the beers produced by the many breweries which surrounded Manchester. It was known as 'fighting beer.' He would always travel the extra mile to find a Chester's house. Some people become overly sentimental when drunk, my father became aggressive. He would fall out with fellow drinkers and then be banned from that particular pub. It also created problems at work. He was sometimes sent home by his printing bosses for being too drunk, and on several occasions suspended – and these were notoriously tolerant (supine, some said) employers. His union, NATSOPA, would then jump to his defence and he would be re-instated. He survived a final warning, and was to work, but more intermittently, until his retirement.

He loved to sing old Irish songs. We might be at the neighbouring house of an aunt or uncle, perhaps celebrating a birthday, when he would launch into *Danny Boy*, which was his favourite, or *I'll take you Home again Kathleen*, and then, as a finale, *If you ever go across the Sea to Ireland*. He comes to mind vividly whenever I hear '… the pipes, the pipes are calling'. He never sang in the presence of my grandmother. She hated to see him drunk, and he kept well out of her way. I once heard her admonish him for the fact that he no longer went to Mass. And I remember his response. 'I see those women,' he mentioned some names, 'lining up to receive Holy Communion, looking pious, and I know where they were last night, and what they were up to.' His cure for a hangover was to break two eggs into a mug, add vinegar, salt and pepper, and then down them, raw, in one gulp.

He did have good intensions. But things never quite worked out. It was in the January of the year following my mother's death that he arranged a very special treat, just for me. Manchester United was to play Aston Villa in the third round of the FA Cup at Villa Park in Birmingham. My father was to take me to the game. In Manchester, at that time, Catholics managed, played for, and supported United; Protestants supported City – although my brother Alan, always contrary, said that he was a City supporter. I was a passionate United fan. I had first been taken to see them play in 1944 at City's ground at Maine Road. United were using it as their home ground whilst Old Trafford recovered from bomb damage. The Villa game turned out to be a classic. United scored in the first minute; at half time they were ahead by five goals to one; with ten minutes to go, Villa had fought back and the score was five goals to four; and the final score was six goals to four. United were destined to go on to win the Cup in that year, at a time long before trophy winning had become routine (before the Busby Babes, and long, long before Ferguson) and when City was still the dominant Manchester club. I remember listening to the Cup Final, at the end of the season, on the wireless at Seymour Road and, in my excitement, dropping on the stone kitchen floor one of the plates which I was drying. Not surprisingly, it shattered. However, there was still further drama to unfold at Villa Park; but this time off the pitch.

Together with a number of other schoolboys, I had been lifted over the perimeter wall and deposited on the grass at the side of the touchline from where I had watched the game. There was a capacity crowd with an attendance of more than 80,000, and this was a necessary way of keeping children away from the crush. But at the end of the match I couldn't find my father. As the ground cleared of spectators, I made my way towards the coach park. I threaded through the massed ranks of similar looking vehicles and eventually found the coach in which we had arrived. The driver was waiting for his missing passengers and waited for a little while longer to see if my father might turn up. But we had to leave without him to start the long journey back from Birmingham to Manchester. My father arrived home much, much later. Somewhat the worse for wear.

On another occasion, we were to have some further excitement. My father's eldest sister, my Auntie Cissy (although she had taken to calling herself Miriam) lived in Ostend, together with her Belgian husband, André. He was a steward on the Dover-Ostend ferry. It was summer, and Alan and I were packed off to their home for a very welcome holiday; our first trip abroad. André met our train in London, and looked after us on the crossing. On the return journey, it had been arranged that my father would meet us off the boat train at Victoria Station. We arrived, on time, but could not find him. We stood around for more than an hour, and must have looked anxious – two small boys alone at a main-line station – because a kind lady came to ask if she could help. I explained our predicament, and, with astonishing generosity, she took us in a taxi from Victoria to Euston, and put us on the train to Manchester; fortunately, we already had our return tickets. From London Road Station (now Manchester Piccadilly) we walked to Stephenson Square where we boarded the trolley bus to Clayton. My father arrived several hours later to explain that he had gone to the wrong London railway station. It had become a habit.

My father's other weakness was his inability to manage money – in stark contrast to his mother. Despite his relatively high wages, after a self-indulgent weekend, he would often have to seek a modest loan to tide him over until his next pay-day. I was sometimes the provider of this short term facility, even whilst I was still at school. I was able to do this because of a money-making game which I operated called 'the score'. It was a simple form of lottery based on the number of points scored by Wigan's rugby league football team in its Saturday game. Each Sunday morning I would cut out 50 slips of paper, the scores, and write on them each of the numbers nought to 50 (excluding the number one). The scores would then be folded and put into a tin box. After Mass, I would visit the homes of various aunts and uncles, including my maternal grandparents – there had been a slight reconciliation after my mother's death – and other neighbours, offering the scores at two pennies each; the winner – the one drawing the number which equated to Wigan's score at the next Saturday game – would receive a prize of five shillings. If I sold all the scores, my takings would be eight shillings and four pence, which meant a profit of three shillings and four pence; a sizeable weekly sum for a 12-year-old boy. But sometimes I did better than that. Wigan was a prolifically high-scoring team. Several times each season they would score in excess of 50 points. On those occasions, I would have the additional profit of the five shillings prize money to add to my three shillings and four pence. The 'score money' was the fund which would sometimes be used to help my father survive until his Friday pay-day. But it was always back in my hands by Saturday morning.

It was many years later, when I had been long established in business in London, that I remember spending an early evening with my father in the bar at Manchester's Piccadilly Hotel. I had recently acquired a children's book publishing company whose offices were in Lever Street, quite close to Piccadilly, and which now brought me back to Manchester from time to time. This particular evening, it must have been in the late 1970s, perhaps the year before my father's death, we were sitting at a side-table when my father saw an immediately recognisable figure standing at the bar. It was Manchester City's manager, Malcolm Allison, in his trademark long overcoat, a match for my father's Crombie, and wide-brimmed hat. My father became a little agitated. 'Do you know him?' he asked. My father assumed that, because my name had appeared in the papers once or twice, I must know every important person, and that they must know me. I said that I did not know Malcolm Allison, and reminded my father that Allison was City and that we were United. 'But, I'd like to meet him,' my father said. I went to the bar. 'I know, Mr. Allison, that you must hear this all the time,' I said, 'but my dad would be very privileged to meet you.' He came to our table, said hello to my father, and could not have been more charming. But I knew that the next day my father would be telling his drinking pals, 'I met that Malcolm Allison last night. 'E's not that special.' Because that is how my dad was.

When I left Xaverian College, there had been little attempt at careers guidance. I had worked in the summer holidays digging drainage trenches at a market garden on Ashton Moss; I had helped with postal deliveries at Christmas time – which was surprisingly well paid, and which presented a first brush with stardust when I delivered letters to John Aston (the Manchester United right back in the 1948 Cup winning team) at his sports shop on the New Road; and I had helped

35

to sell copies of the Empire News (a Sunday paper then available on Saturday nights with the latest football results) from a strategic street corner pitch at the Old Road end of Viaduct Street. But now I had to seek my first proper job. I reported to the labour exchange in Lower Mosley Street in central Manchester. I was sent straightaway to the offices of a cotton manufacturer, who were looking for a clerk. Haslam's Ltd had its head office and warehouse in Quay Street, which was off Deansgate – the other end of Deansgate from Kendal Milne. The Manchester Opera House was its immediate neighbour, and some years later Granada was to build its television studios further down the street. I was interviewed by the company secretary, offered a job in the forwarding department, and was to start the following week.

Mr Butterworth was my manager, and my main task was to assemble the various documents for each transaction – bills of lading, letters of credit, pro-forma invoices – and summarise them on a covering docket. I would then have to go to the offices of a director and of the company secretary to obtain their signatures as the final authorisation. We dealt only with the company's export business. The customers for the fine cottons were spread throughout the world, but were mainly in the old British Empire, with the British West Indies, East Africa, and Australia being particularly important markets. The work was interesting, and I enjoyed basking in the reflected glory of those who had concluded these transactions in such exotic locations. Never dreaming for a moment that I might one day visit any of them. At Mr Butterworth's suggestion, I enrolled at a college of further education for a night-school course which could lead to a qualification which, he had said, would be helpful in progressing my career.

I had few friends and little social activity; work and night-school became the central part of my life. Moving from Beswick to Clayton, to Abergele Sanatorium, then to Woodhouse Park and back to Clayton had made it difficult to establish firm friendships. I cannot remember ever even speaking to another boy – or girl – in the whole time we lived in Woodhouse Park. And the move from St. Anne's to Xaverian, and, crucially, the time away in hospital, meant that I had developed no real school friends. At Xaverian, after TB, I had been treated like a delicate flower, and had been excused games, which I am not sure was strictly necessary. So, I played no sport – which was to become so important to me later in life – and never learned to swim. I also never learned to ride a bike. A bonus of missing games was that I had a weekly outing with my rather smart cousin, Angela. She was Auntie Cissy's only daughter and she worked as a receptionist at the imposing Midland Hotel. Perhaps as a result, she was much more sophisticated than anybody else I knew. I would meet her at the hotel, and, whilst the rest of my class was playing football, we would go for a walk in Platt Fields if it was a fine day, or for a coffee at the Kardomah Café in St. Anne's Square if it was raining.

In Seymour Road we received a visit from a Jesuit priest, who talked to me in the presence of my father and my grandmother. He was under the impression that I was a likely candidate for the priesthood. He was quickly disabused of that idea, but he left the house happy in the knowledge that my spiritual guidance was in the very capable hands of the brothers of St. Francis Xavier. However, I was soon to stop going to confession and to Mass. My faith had never been strong and the whole exercise just seemed to be pointless. Perhaps, it was simply that it was much more comfortable to stay in bed on a Sunday morning rather than to get up to go to church. My grandmother was disappointed, but she slowly got used to the idea. Her views had certainly softened as she had aged, because, at one time, she would not have had anybody in the house who did not go to Mass. The priests had lost their battle, but perhaps not. Because, as they would argue, once a Catholic, always a Catholic; a Catholic is for life – or even longer. A former Catholic is an oxymoron. Technically, I was a lapsed Catholic. The Jesuits have much to answer for.

I now sometimes went to the Congregational Church Hall for its Saturday social evenings, which included dancing. Not because of some newly found enthusiasm for a new religious experience, but because of its convenience. It was situated at the end of Seymour Road. And there was little else on offer. It was there that I met another boy, Peter, and his older sister. It might be that they first asked me there. They lived in a posher part of Clayton – everything is relative – on the other side of North Road, which was at the opposite end of Seymour Road from the New Road. Their parents actually owned the house – owner occupied, although I am not sure that I was aware of the expression at the time. They also owned a music shop on the New Road. I was invited back to their home, where their mother provided tea, and this was repeated several times. Peter's mother thought that I was good for him because, so she said, I was clever, and went to a good school. She thought I might provide some motivation for her lack-lustre son. I am sure that she had some doubts about my background; I came from the wrong side of North Road. And, of course, I was a Catholic. My grandmother, who had not met Peter, said that we must reciprocate. He was invited, by me, for Sunday afternoon tea. My grandmother set the table carefully and the boiled ham, bread and best butter, and slices of slab cake made an attractive spread. But Peter did not appear. He had simply forgotten. It was probably not as important to his family as it was to mine.

Another friend, Alan, was a trainee men's hairdresser who worked in an old-fashioned barber's shop near Strangeways Prison. He was later to play an unexpectedly pivotal role in my career. Our Saturday night excursions took us as far as the dancehall at Belle Vue; which was a little more exciting than the Congregational Church Hall. We went once to a central Manchester jazz club, and, at Easter, we went to the fairground at Daisy Nook. It did not amount to very much. We were not yet into girlfriends – or perhaps it was simply that they were not into us. I already felt as if I were at a dead end. Life at home was not easy (the family was not prone to show emotion), the charms of Haslam's forwarding office had begun to fade, and my social life (which I never really thought of as such) was almost non-existent. Looming on the horizon was National Service. I decided to anticipate its inevitability by paying a visit to the RAF recruitment centre.

I do not know why I chose the air force rather than the army. However, I met the recruitment officer and he highlighted the attractions of a regular engagement. It would mean an initial commitment of three years rather than the mandatory two years of National Service. This initial term could be extended. It would mean a better opportunity to develop a career. And it paid more. I had made the appointment because of my feeling of restlessness, without any clear idea about my future, and with the knowledge that I would, in any event, shortly be called up for National Service. At the back of my mind had been the thought that a long term career in the Royal Air Force might be a possibility. So, I was easily persuaded. One opportunity which we discussed together was that I could be part of an educational unit which, amongst other things, would advise other recruits on their own career opportunities. The officer thought that I would quickly be promoted. A rank as high as a warrant officer was mentioned. I doubt that the possibility of anything more ambitious than that – a commissioned officer! – ever remotely entered into either of our minds. It already sounded pretty good to me. At the end of the interview, I had agreed to take up a three year regular engagement as an airman. Within a matter of weeks, I received my travel warrant and my instructions. I was to report to Cardington for induction and training.

III
LIFE IN A SANATORIUM

The night before I was to leave for Cardington, it was September 1953, my father took me into one of his regular pubs to have a drink with him. He still did not frequent the pubs of Clayton, but had continued to give his support to the pubs of Beswick and Ancoats. The Viaduct Inn was a traditional and fairly basic, sawdust-on-the-floor, beer house. It was only a few strides away from where we had lived at 94 Viaduct Street. I had spent many hours waiting for my father outside pubs, but this was the first time I had been inside. My Auntie Kathleen had warned me of the perils – evils even – of public houses, and pointed to my father as her justification. 'You don't want to be like your Dad,' she would say. Technically, by law, I was still not quite old enough to drink alcohol in a public house, but my father reasoned that if I was old enough to join the armed forces, then that was good enough for him. We sat together for a little more than an hour. I slowly drank – nursed – my first pint of bitter, it was not Chester's; my father did rather better. I then left him with one of his drinking companions and caught the trolley bus back to Seymour Road, to prepare for my big day, tomorrow. I was three months short of my eighteenth birthday. I felt happier than I had felt for a long time.

When I boarded the ten o'clock train for Euston at London Road Station, I met several other recruits, who were on the same journey to Cardington. The recruiting office might have booked a compartment, or perhaps just adjoining seats. One of them had a pack of playing cards. A game of five-card brag was suggested. My father had taught me cribbage, and I had played brag a couple of times at Xaverian. So, along the way, I had picked up the rudiments of some card and board games. I was not very good, but the others were much worse. And I was a quick learner. I was soon very much in pocket, and, at about the mid-point of our journey to London, the game was abandoned. My new companions had suddenly lost their enthusiasm. Whilst we had been playing, a girl of a similar age to ours had been watching the game – a kibitzer – a word I later came to know from the world of bridge. She also had a travel warrant, but she was making the reverse journey. She was now returning home, having given up on the idea of a military career with the WRAF. The initial training at her induction centre in Lancashire had not been to her taste. We seemed to hit it off. Perhaps she was impressed by my card playing skills; perhaps not. It turned out that she was a great jazz enthusiast. I used the experience of my one visit to a jazz club in Manchester to suggest that we had a shared interest. As we approached London we exchanged addresses, although all that I could offer was RAF Cardington. I had probably talked with her, at a single sitting, for longer than I had with any previous girl of my age. At Euston, we parted, and I boarded the train for Cardington in Bedfordshire. We wrote to each other, but we never met again. It had been an eventful journey.

As we arrived at RAF Cardington, we were greeted by the sight of a World War Two Spitfire mounted on a plinth at the entrance gate. My pulses quickened. Part of the welcoming process at the reception centre included a cursory form of medical examination. It mainly involved form filling and box ticking but there was also a chest X-ray. It strikes me now, but did not at the time, that it was odd that the medical did not take place in Manchester, when an unnecessary journey could have been avoided should a problem arise. It was to prove to be a costly mistake. After lights-out at the end of my first day as an airman (as I thought) few of us were in a mood for settling down. There was an air of excitement. All of that day's entry was in the same barrack-room. Most were from the Manchester area. Disembodied voices would declaim the merits of the various districts of the city – and of its football teams. I found myself defending my own poor, beleaguered streets. Much to my surprise, I was one of the more vocal contributors. I was noted for being shy, not gregarious. Perhaps it was the effect of talking in the anonymity of the dark. Whatever the reason, I was beginning to enjoy myself.

The following morning, I was singled out from the rest of the intake and asked to report to the sick bay. There I was told that there was a problem with my X-ray, but that it was probably technical. A second photograph was taken and I was asked to sit and await the results. The technician re-appeared with a frown on his face. There was still a problem. There was an apparent shadow on the left lung. He asked if I had recently had a cold. My answer was a little inconclusive, 'I often had colds.' I suppose I was anxious to give him the answer he wanted. Anyway, it was good enough for him. 'You probably have a build-up of phlegm on your chest which is causing the shadow on the lung,' he explained, 'but we can soon deal with that.' The proposed solution was for me to lie across the side of a bed whilst an orderly enthusiastically pummelled my back as I coughed and hawked into a metal dish. This procedure was repeated later in the day. My belongings had been transferred from the barrack-room and I was now properly installed in the sick bay until they could get a satisfactory X-ray and release me back into the mainstream. The following day, after yet more pummelling, I had another X-ray. There was no change. The technician and orderly were looking a little defeatist. Yet they still remained anxious not to let this new recruit go. The medical officer was consulted. The TB history was mentioned. It was decided, with some reluctance – and nobody was more disappointed than me – that I was to be transferred to the RAF hospital at Wroughton for further investigation. As I travelled alone in the ambulance from Bedfordshire to Wiltshire, I reflected on my predicament. I did not feel particularly unwell, but, if I was sick, I could not believe that the very vigorous pounding on my back with hard fists would have helped. It seemed a basic and primitive policy born of desperation. And my career in the Royal Air Force appeared, at the very least, to be in jeopardy.

My arrival at Wroughton was to lead to some embarrassment for the hospital hierarchy. From an examination of the contents of one of the sputum boxes, which were for a time to be my constant companion on the bedside table, it was established that my tuberculosis had returned. As the medical records put it, 'the sputum was positive for tubercle bacilli on direct film.' This time it was more serious than the previous episode of primary tuberculosis as, in addition to the shadow on the lower part of the left lung, there were also cavities caused by the activity of the bacilli – which would certainly not have been helped by the pummelling. And the bacilli were still active as the sputum had tested positive.

The problem for the hospital authorities was that I was still a civilian but in an RAF hospital. It was now clear that my service career had ended before it had begun. The RAF had an obvious duty to care for me whilst I was in its custody, but its main concern was – how to get rid of me? Negotiations with the National Health Service in Manchester took several weeks, before it was possible to find a place in one of its hospitals. In the meantime, I was being looked after – very well looked after, with a daily bottle of Guinness – in one of the hospital wards. The other patients, who were airmen and non-commissioned officers, took great delight in encouraging my insubordination, as, being a civilian, I was not subject to military discipline from the parading, properly commissioned sisters. Eventually, I was told that I was to be transferred to Westmoreland Sanatorium. But the continuing responsibilities and costs for the Royal Air Force were not yet at an end.

The day of my departure from Wroughton started in high drama verging on farce. I was carried on a stretcher, under escort, into an ambulance which delivered me to Swindon railway station. As the stretcher-bearer bore me across the street and into the station concourse, concerned passers-by gave me encouraging and sympathetic glances, and one even patted my legs through the covering blanket. A whole coach of the train had been reserved and on each of the windows was a sign dramatically proclaiming 'Infectious Disease.' As soon as we were in the railway carriage, I left the stretcher and took a normal position on a seat by the window. I was perfectly capable of walking under my own steam. There were just the two of us (my escort was an RAF orderly) in that whole ghostly carriage on the long journey from Swindon to Crewe. It was like an eerie scene from *Nineteen Eighty-Four*. At Crewe, we changed trains for Grange-over-Sands, and again there was the reserved coach and the spooky

'Infectious Disease' posters. But this time we dispensed with the stretcher. At Grange-over-Sands, a waiting ambulance took us across the Lancashire border into Westmoreland and to the small village of Meathop where the sanatorium was situated, and where I was to spend the next year of my life. My escort was given a bed for the night and returned to base the following morning. I am sure that the Royal Air Force was glad to see the back of me.

Westmoreland Sanatorium was in an isolated position at the southern borders of the Lake District. It was surrounded by rugged countryside where hill farmers struggled to make a living. Throughout the day, and it sometimes seemed the night as well, the bleating of the sheep was a constant background noise. The hospital's patients were all from the Manchester area. Whereas Abergele Sanatorium had looked after the children, Westmoreland Sanatorium looked after the adults. Both catered for tubercular Mancunians. Arrangements similar to those at Abergele existed for visitors; a coach left Manchester city centre each Sunday morning. I had visitors on perhaps six to ten occasions during my stay, as both my grandmother and my father still found it difficult to make the journey on a regular basis. Sundays were not usually happy days for me. Of even greater importance than visiting day, however, was the weekly doctor's round. On first arrival at the hospital, patients would usually be confined to bed – particularly if still testing positive for tuberculosis. They would not be allowed to leave their beds even to go to the lavatory; which had its obvious inconveniencies. If I ever again suffer the indignity of needing to use a bedpan, I can well imagine contemplating suicide. After a period of immobility, and assuming some improvement (again the sputum examination was crucial, as a positive reading would keep the patient in bed indefinitely) there would be a gradual progression of status. The first step was being allowed to visit the bathroom. Then for the patient to be able, each day, to leave his bed for a specific period of time – first one hour, then two hours, four hours, seven hours, and, finally, all day. Each Monday morning, the doctor, on his round, would review the progress of each patient. Most often there would be little more than a cursory, 'Good morning, how are you' – 'Good,' and then he would move on. He was a man of few words, and little emotion. But the occasions when he would pause and say, for example, 'I think that we can now raise the one hour to two hours' created a sense of joy and happiness which, to an outside observer, would seem totally disproportionate for so small a change in routine. It was a tangible sign on the road to recovery.

The wards were organised into cubicles of two beds each, with open access to a veranda. As with Abergele, beds were pushed out onto the veranda in most weathers. There was now, however, one critical difference in the treatment of tuberculosis. This was the development of the 'wonder drug', streptomycin. In its early form, streptomycin had been used to treat George Orwell (Eric Blair), but Orwell had to abandon the medication after a reaction and he died, at the age of 46, in 1950. By 1953, it had been refined and developed into a three-way mixture of antibiotics. Together with the programme of mass X-rays for the crucial early detection of infection, which was later introduced, streptomycin offered a highly successful cure to a devastating disease which, as I could testify, was still rampant. I was one of the early, lucky beneficiaries. My treatment with the drug had started in Wroughton and it now continued at Meathop. I had injections twice a day. My bottom soon felt as if it had been used as a pin-cushion. It was painful. Very! But it was effective. My sputum was soon no longer testing positive. The bacilli had ceased to cause further damage to my lungs and recuperation could begin. But, in December 1953, that was still a little way off.

A long period of time in a hospital is a quite different experience from the more typical hospital stay which might involve, for example, an operation, a short period of recovery, and then a return home. That typical stay had a specific objective with a fairly clearly defined time-span. The situation in which I found myself was one in which it was difficult to contemplate the future, because it was impossible to know how long it would take to recover my health. Some patients had already spent more than a year of their lives in, or close to, their beds. Some were never to return home. It was like being in a prison with a long but indeterminate sentence. Doctors were not helpful in giving guidance as to how long things might take. Perhaps they had too often been disappointed; and their experience with streptomycin was still quite new. I do not remember ever feeling particularly ill, or even suffering pain – except from the medication. But then, of course, tuberculosis is a wasting disease. In the still dark of the night I would sometimes think that I might die. But I had no real justification for such thoughts.

Patients quickly become institutionalised. Routine, however trivial, becomes important. Breakfast, lunch, tea and supper assume a disproportionate significance. We looked forward to the twice daily visits of the nurse for the checking of temperature and pulse and the administration of medication (even the hypodermic needle provided a distraction – but not quite so welcome); to the journey to the radiologist for the periodic X-rays; to Sundays for those expecting visitors; and, of course, to the crucial Monday doctor's round. These were the highlights of life in the hospital bubble.

There were no telephones, and no television; just reading materials – newspapers, books and magazines – and headphones for the wireless. I do not remember ever seeing alcohol on the wards; not like the Guinness at Wroughton. I drank alcohol only twice in my long stay (I have since made up for it). The first occasion was on the Christmas Eve of 1953. Four of us put on some outdoor clothes over our pyjamas and crept out of the ward late at night to undertake a two mile walk to the nearest public house. There, we drank beer and played darts for perhaps an hour before returning, unobserved, to our beds. At that time, I had been confined to my bed, at Wroughton and at Meathop together, for almost three months and must have been very weak. It was a risky and irresponsible thing to do on a dark and bitterly cold night. My father might have been proud. But then perhaps he might not.

To my chagrin, I did not read many books (again, I have now more than made up for that), but newspapers I read assiduously. This was to take an unusual turn. I was, from home, vaguely familiar with newspaper racing pages. My father was known to bet on the horses, and big races such as the Derby and the Grand National had always aroused great interest and excitement with all the family members placing at least one small bet. Now, I began to study the subject with an academic intensity. I read the racing news in all the newspapers. I compiled lists of the previous results for the participating horses in each race, gathered together clues with regard to current form, and established the odds available from bookmakers. I compared the different views of the various tipsters. I even read the specialist horse-racing press. I accumulated all the data in my little black notebook. It became an obsession. A new interest.

This interest had been encouraged by the fact that a fellow patient had been a back street bookmaker in Manchester and was now happy to make a book, take bets, in the hospital ward – probably illegally. It was from him that I borrowed copies of the *Sporting Life* and the *Sporting Chronicle*. I became a regular customer, placing small bets each day. I had some success, which I assumed was due to my skill and dedication. It was more likely beginner's luck. I did come close to one major coup. In my researches, I came across a horse, Churchtown, which was down to run in both the Leopardstown Chase (in Ireland) and the Grand National. I obtained attractive odds from my new best friend, the bookmaker, and placed a small each-way bet for the horse to be placed in the first three in both races – a double. Although the stake was small, it could multiply dramatically if the bet was successful. Churchtown won the Irish race at a canter. In the pre-race betting for the Grand National, Churchtown now became one of the favourites, having initially been an outsider. The bookmaker was looking anxious. We listened together to the race on the wireless. Churchtown was amongst the leaders and cleared all the fences. But it finished fourth. The bet had failed by the smallest of margins. I have never considered myself a gambler. I am not, unlike many people who are gamblers, superstitious. I now play bridge, but bridge I consider to be a game of skill rather than a game of chance. Shortly after the Churchtown episode, my enthusiasm seemed to wane. Perhaps it had run its natural course; and, as my health was improving, I was now able to move around more freely, and even to contemplate the possibility of going home. The interest in horse racing died and was never to be resurrected.

At the time I was studying the racing press, I was also reading another form of specialist publication. I had written to the girl I had met on the train from Manchester to Euston, and she had replied with warmth and sympathy. We became pen-pals. From our discussion on the train, she had assumed a shared degree of interest in jazz which was not then, on my part, justified. She sent to me, each week, a copy of the *Melody Maker* and the *New Musical Express* to feed what she thought was my appetite for all things jazz. She was seriously keen – on jazz, that is. It was at the time of the dispute between the American and British musicians' unions. The British union would not allow American jazz musicians to play in England unless there was a reciprocal arrangement for British musicians to play in America. Unfortunately, although British jazz enthusiasts were desperate to see and hear the American jazz stars, the American public had no interest in supporting British musicians, however talented they might be, of whom they had never heard. This was all covered at length in my music magazines. There was a stand-off which was to last for several years, but there was one chink which was found in the British armour which came about whilst I was at Meathop. It was established that the American air force base at Burtonwood was considered to be American territory. The Stan Kenton Orchestra, of which I had become a fan, was booked to play there, and this single event was allowed to go ahead. I was now listening, most nights, to jazz from the American Forces Network on the wireless and I was able to hear the entire Kenton concert. Fantastic! Unlike horse racing, jazz has remained an important interest. Thanks to my pen-pal.

Since the beginning of 1954, the sputum tests, thanks to streptomycin, had been consistently negative, and I no longer had my daily injections. Gradually, I was able to take some exercise, as I was allowed more time away from my bed. There was, however, one major obstacle, which I had still to overcome, before it would be possible to return to what I hoped would be a normal life. Although the disease had cleared from my lungs, the bacilli had left their mark. The lower part of my left lung was scarred and pitted with cavities which could provide a host for future infections unless treated. There were two possible solutions. The first was to remove the bottom half of the lung – a lobectomy. This would require major surgery, with the possible additional removal of one or more ribs to provide access to the lung. A neighbouring patient had suffered this procedure and did not make a full recovery. I did not see him again. The second possibility was a measure described as an artificial pneumothorax. This involved detaching the lung from the ribcage, to which it had become adhered from the effusions of the tubercular sores, and then depressing the lung so that it was effectively folded over. This would encourage, over a period of time, the formation of scar tissue which would cover the cavities and thus reduce the risk of infection. This was the procedure which we agreed upon. It was carried out successfully under a local anaesthetic. The way in which the lung was depressed was by the injection of air through the chest wall. Normal physical movement would slowly dissipate the air and it was therefore necessary to replace it twice weekly by further injections. This became a new part of my routine and when I eventually left Meathop, I had to visit the Manchester Chest Hospital to continue the treatment.

I was getting close to my hospital discharge. I had left the main ward and now occupied one of a number of tiny chalets which were reserved for patients who were allowed to be away from their beds for the whole of the day. I felt very privileged. I was able to go for short walks in an adjacent wood. There was a nearby sister hospital for tubercular women, and there were rumours of trysts in the woodlands. I was not one of the lucky ones. I did have one final excursion. It was the custom to allow patients close to release to visit Grange-over-Sands on a Saturday morning in a hospital vehicle. This provided only the second experience of alcohol in my long stay – the first had been on the reckless outing on Christmas Eve. Two of us went on the trip. We visited the British Legion, where we had been told we had honorary rights, sank a pint, and played snooker. Freedom beckoned.

One of the senior doctors came to bid me farewell. He told me that I must remember that I was still an invalid; that I would not be able to lead a normal life; and that I must not, for example, attempt to run for a bus. Reflecting on these cautionary words, I set off on my journey back to Manchester. It had been a year since I had arrived at RAF Cardington with such high hopes.

IV
WHAT DOES
AN ACCOUNTANT DO?

Back in Manchester, it was the autumn of 1954, I was soon, again, at a loose end. I was still, in the vernacular of those times, 'under the doctor'. I was considered unfit for work, and, of course, had to go to the chest clinic in Moss Side – not too far from the Xaverian College – twice each week for an air re-fill. Nobody seemed to know when I would be able to resume work, and it was not even clear as to what work I would be able to undertake. Certainly nothing too strenuous. I was not short of money as the sick pay seemed more than adequate – even generous – for my modest means. I did not feel unwell – my consistent litany – and I was impatient for my life to start again. I would sometimes get the trolley bus into Stephenson Square, walk to the Littlewoods store in Market Street, and idly listen to the music – usually the current popular hits – in the record department. I might have a sandwich for lunch – although lunch did not seem important in those days – and then drift slowly over towards Victoria Station and the Strangeways area where my friend Alan (we had stayed in touch whilst I was away, and he had once paid a visit to Meathop) still worked in the same barber's shop. It was there that my fortunes took a dramatic change.

Alan's boss was very talkative – one of the important skills of his trade. He knew something about my background from Alan, and I had already been in his shop several times, and had even had a haircut. He mentioned a regular customer by the name of Joe Morris. 'Joe,' he said, 'is always complaining that he can never find good people' – *plus ça change*. 'You are supposed to be quick with figures,' he continued, 'you should speak to him.' Joe Morris was a chartered accountant in private practice. I had little idea what a chartered accountant was, or what an accountant did. I have mentioned already that careers guidance had not been one of Xaverian College's strong points. As I was not yet able to work, there seemed little point in pursuing his suggestion, but Alan's boss was persuasive. 'Perhaps you can work part-time,' he said, 'and, anyway, there can be no harm in having a meeting.' It was agreed that he would raise the matter with Mr Morris when he next came in. In due course, an appointment was made for me to see him.

I arrived at the offices of J. Morris & Co., at the junction of Princess Street and Albert Square, opposite the Town Hall, at three o'clock on a clear late autumn afternoon. It was some weeks before my nineteenth birthday. The offices occupied the second floor of a Victorian building whose main occupant was an insurance company. I pressed a button for the bell outside the reception window. It was not working. I tapped on the window to announce my presence, and it was opened by a middle-aged man, with a pencil tucked behind his ear, who I later found to be the book-keeper and cashier. He would often tease me, after I had become an established member of the firm, at the nature of my arrival. 'There was a timid knock at the window,' he would say, and then, this he would mimic in a rough Manchester accent, 'I've cum about the part-time job.'

I was ushered in to meet Mr Morris in his smoke-filled room. He was always to be Mr Morris to me during the nearly six years in which I worked for him, and when I was to meet him at the funeral of a mutual friend, 30 years later, he was still 'Mr Morris'. Joe Morris was a gruff Lancastrian who hailed from Radcliffe, to the north of Manchester, but now lived in Lytham St. Anne's, an upmarket neighbour of Blackpool, from where he commuted each day by train. He wore a traditional, but rather shiny, three-piece suit, was a chain smoker of small cigars, and would not leave the offices without his overcoat and bowler hat. He must have taken to me, because he offered me a job, and asked if I could start the following Monday morning.

Mr Morris understood that I was still not 'signed-off' by my doctors to start work, that I was not certain of my stamina, and that I still had to visit the chest clinic twice each week. The solution which he proposed was that I should work each day for as long as I could, and then stop when I felt tired. I would not be on the formal payroll, but he would pay me three pounds each week from petty cash. This would all be reviewed if I survived a trial period, and when my medical status was clarified. This strikes me now as being a somewhat irregular arrangement, but there was no easy alternative. I was still receiving sick-pay, as, officially, I was not allowed to work. But now, I was also to be paid for my part-time employment; possibly, an early example of benefit fraud. Fortunately for my criminal record, it was not to continue for too long.

Mr Morris was the firm's sole principal, and the other main staff members were another chartered accountant – recently qualified – two senior audit clerks, a junior audit clerk, and an articled clerk. I was to be – for the trial, probationary period – the second junior audit clerk. Not that I knew what this meant, or what the duties entailed.

In the large firms of professional accountants, there are specialist departments for the different elements of an accountant's role – audit, tax, consultancy, insolvency, investigations, and corporate finance. In a small practice such as J. Morris & Co., the staff member who had responsibility for a particular client would handle every aspect of that client's affairs. This would usually involve the audit of the firm's or company's books of account, the preparation of the final accounts, the calculation of the tax liability, and then the agreement of that liability with the Inland Revenue. The role was that of a generalist rather than a specialist.

Small business enterprises, perhaps a sole trader with a single high street shop, would often have no books to audit. He would simply dump several shoe boxes of invoices and bank statements, from which the accounts had to be prepared, onto the poor audit clerk's desk. It was described as preparing accounts from incomplete records. Some of the records were very incomplete and had to involve a degree of fabrication. In this environment, an aspiring accountant – this was not yet me – had an unusual variety of tasks and experiences, and had the satisfaction of advising and dealing directly with a wide range of clients. This was not possible in the big accountancy firms where the work was compartmentalised, and where an accountant could spend several months engaged in the routine audit of the accounts of just one huge client.

In the first few weeks of my new work, much of my time was spent in 'calling over' – this was checking entries in the client's traditional double-entry book-keeping system. Sales and purchase invoices would be checked with the day books, and then the entries in the day books and in the cash book would be checked with the sales and purchase ledgers, in which were listed the accounts of the client's customers and suppliers. The figures would be 'ticked' in ink of the special colour which was being used for that particular year of the audit. A different coloured ink would be used for each year. It was not then clear to me what the purpose was – I just made sure that the figures were the same in both ledgers. It was to be some time before I was to become involved in the intricacies of the trial balance and the preparation of the profit and loss account and balance sheet; particularly making sure that both sides matched – it was not good enough to accept a small difference of just a few pounds as that might cloak compensating errors of perhaps millions. Both sides of the trial balance and the balance sheet had to add up to the same figure – exactly! A story, perhaps apocryphal, was told of an audit clerk who was unable to balance the books because, at the head of the trial balance, he had entered the date, and then added in the date figures to his total.

Amongst Mr Morris's portfolio of clients were some interesting audits. Samuels Gowns was situated in King Street, which was then an elegant street in central Manchester leading down to Kendal Milne in Deansgate. It claimed to be the premier fashion store in Manchester – and beyond. It was owned and managed by the Samuels family; a brother and his two sisters. They believed that their emporium was a match for any comparable store which might be found in London's Bond Street or Knightsbridge. Mr Louis was to be found at the front of the house, but his formidable sisters had established a rule of terror in the work-rooms and back offices. Checking the books in an inner sanctum, we were privileged to have a front row seat in a theatre of haut couture. Sadly, and all too frequently, we would also witness a poor seamstress trembling at the approach of one of the sisters – perhaps Miss Esther. The sisters were very particular about the audit clerks who examined their books. They were concerned to protect the identity of their clientele, and their frock and hat buying habits. They had been known to telephone Mr Morris to ask for the removal of an auditor who was not to their taste. When, later, Mr Morris had a Nigerian articled clerk, he was never able to summon up the courage to send him on the Samuels audit. Perhaps it was just natural self-preservation, as the Samuels' audit fee made a significant contribution to the always precarious finances of his small accountancy practice.

Another client company occupied a cotton mill in Oldham, a town which was some miles to the north and east of Manchester. It was an audit with a degree of poignancy. It had once been a significant cotton weaving company, but now the machinery was stilled – much of it already removed – and parts of the ground floor of this enormous building, and several of the outbuildings, were let to local tradesmen. The other floors were empty, and the echoing footsteps, and the realisation that its bustling past was never to return, created a sad and eerie atmosphere. The mill owner was a Mr Rose, and he was the kindest and most courteous man I had so far met. He had once been a cotton baron. Now, he sat each day in his disproportionately large office dealing with more mundane matters, and managing his much diminished fortune. But he was always cheerful. We would occupy a nearby annexe, into which we would carry enormous ledgers which were packed with page after page of figures which represented the history of the company from its thriving successful years as a cotton mill. The figures for the current year covered just a few pages, and were confined simply to rental income from the new tenants, and investment income from the cash deposits.

An audit which had once extended over several weeks, was now completed in a matter of days. I enjoyed travelling on the train from Manchester to Oldham. It seemed like a real outing. On one occasion, the new Nigerian articled clerk joined me on the audit. We went into a local shop to buy sandwiches for lunch. Two elderly ladies behind the counter could not take their eyes away from the face of my colleague. They had not seen a black man before. At the end of the audit, Mr Rose would call me into his office, thank me for my work, shake my hand, and give me two large five pound notes – a sizeable sum in those days, and a practice which would raise eyebrows in today's environment.

We audited the accounts of other companies engaged in motor trading and clothing manufacture, several belonging to the same families, which were based in Prestwich to the north of Manchester. There were no public company audits. Most of Mr Morris's clients were Jewish, which he was not, although his name could be seen to be ambiguous. In the office we would sometimes speculate that it might suit a number of the clients to have a non-Jewish accountant so that their affairs were less likely to become more widely known within the Jewish community. But I have run ahead of myself.

Within days of starting work at J. Morris & Co., the part-time job had morphed into a full-time job. I enjoyed the work and the routine, and did not want to appear too different from my new colleagues. It seemed easier to start and finish the day with them, and I did not find it in the least tiring. The one difference, of course, was that I was still attending the chest clinic for 'fresh' air. It was on one of those visits, in February 1955, some three months after starting with Mr Morris, that I was told that a small left pleural effusion had developed. In layman's terms, this was fluid on the lung, and it was being aggravated by the regular infusions of air. The artificial pneumothorax had to be abandoned, but its job had been done. Sufficient scar tissue had formed over the damaged part of the lung. The consultant agreed that I could now be declared fit for work, and that I could begin, again, to lead a normal life. I was determined to contradict the final dispiriting prognosis of the doctor at Westmoreland Sanatorium. I remained under the supervision of the Manchester Chest Clinic until July 1960, when it was confirmed that I remained symptom free. There was to be no recurrence of infection. However, even today – 60 years later – should I have a routine chest X-ray, the radiographer, if unaware of my history, will rush to her superiors to express her concern, as she sees evidence of that history on the chest film.

My return to Manchester from Meathop had not been to the home I had left a year earlier in Seymour Road, but to a house in an adjacent street, Pennell Street, literally, around the corner. It was a two up and two down house, with a lavatory in the back yard, and a front door which opened directly onto the pavement. Very much like Viaduct Street. It was not clear to me why the change had been made, but I assume that a lower rent for a smaller house must have been an important consideration. When I entered the house for the first time, I saw that my grandfather was very sick, and had his bed in the downstairs front room. My grandmother had long prophesied that he would not make old bones and she was about to be proved right. He was coughing up blood and what appeared to be fragments of his lungs. The detritus of war, as the mustard gas took its final toll. Or it might have been cancer, a disease which in those days was rarely mentioned. In any event, he survived for only two more weeks. My second experience of death and my second funeral.

The paucity of my social life was about the same as it was before my decision to join the Royal Air Force. My tastes in jazz had changed from the traditional jazz which I had enjoyed on my single visit to the jazz club in Cross Street. The influence of my hospital pen-pal and the nocturnal wireless at Meathop had converted me to modern jazz. Some Saturday nights I went, with my barber friend, to the Alhambra Palais on the Old Road, where they featured big-band modern jazz. And I was fortunate to be at the launch of Ronnie Scott's first jazz orchestra at Manchester's High Street baths, little realising at the time what a significant landmark in the history of British jazz that would prove to be.

An important and civilising part of the social fabric of the working class areas of the North of England were the working men's clubs. Their members would include skilled tradesmen and local shopkeepers. They had proper, formal admission procedures, and it was considered an achievement to be accepted as a member. They have now been devastated, and their future threatened, by the smoking ban. Another victim of the law of unintended consequences. London still does not understand the North. My father had never been known to cross the threshold of a working men's club. He preferred the harder drinking environment of the pubs. And he might never have been accepted as a member. They do not seem to have been a natural habitat for Catholics, and it would not have been surprising if the vetting of applicants for membership did not involve a certain degree of discrimination. And, of course, there were social clubs, which served a similar purpose, attached to many of the

Catholic churches. I was twice taken to Clayton Working Men's Club by a friend who was working there as a pianist. I remember the high standards of behaviour and the formal good manners of the members and their guests. Quite different from many of the neighbouring public houses. And they were still having a good time.

I do not remember many sunny days from my childhood. Most days seemed cold and damp and grey. Years later, I returned to those same streets. Apart from the usual impression of how small the houses and streets now seemed compared to the version in my memory, one thing struck me with great force. Looking from Clayton, along the New Road towards Ashton and Stalybridge, a range of hills was outlined on the skyline. It seemed almost within touching distance. They were the Pennines. And yet, in the years in which I had lived there, I had been totally unaware of them. They had been lost in the smoke and haze from the belching chimneys of the mills and factories, and the coal fires of the regiments of terraced houses. This was long before the introduction of the Clean Air Act. Perhaps governments do, sometimes, get things right.

My health history meant that we were again at the top of the Town Hall's waiting list for council houses. After six months in Pennell Street, I was to move again to the South Manchester extremity of Woodhouse Park – but this time together with my grandmother. We left the dark, drab, dreary streets of Clayton and Beswick for the last time; and I was to remain in Woodhouse Park – with a brief intermission – until my marriage five years later.

The decision by my doctors that I was now fit to start work meant that my employment with J. Morris & Co. could be regularised; and that proper consideration could be given to my likely prospects. Mr Morris thought that I had the ability to pursue a successful career in accountancy. To become a chartered accountant it was necessary to enter into articles – a form of apprenticeship. It was the custom for a student who wished to become an articled clerk to pay a premium to the principal, and then to work unpaid for the five year period of the articles. The principal would provide close supervision and advice at work, and would allow generous time away from the office for full time study in the period leading up to the intermediate and final examinations. That, at least, was the concept. But many principals simply used articled clerks as a source of cheap labour, and made little attempt at personal tuition. In any event, articles was not an option for me as I did not have the money to pay a premium and I needed to earn a salary. Mr Morris was sympathetic to my plight, but he was unable to make an exception. He was frank in explaining to me that the benefit – to him – of articled clerks (he was allowed two) was an essential element in the finances of the practice. He could not grant articles to me and also pay a salary, as this would use up one from his quota of two articled clerks. However, there was a possible alternative.

The Institute of Chartered Accountants was the premier accounting body in England and Wales (there was a separate body in Scotland), and it had enormous prestige both here and abroad. There was a story, again perhaps apocryphal, of an accountant in practice in some overseas country who placed the letters ACA (failed) after his name. It seemed that even a failed chartered accountant was better than no chartered accountant at all. And at least it showed that he had been articled and had taken the examinations. There was also a second accountancy body, The Association of

Certified and Corporate Accountants (ACCA). Its members were designated certified accountants and they had the same professional and legal status under the Companies Acts as chartered accountants but did not have quite the same social cachet. There were similar standards for entry, with rigorous examinations, and usually at least a five year period before qualification – but with the crucial difference that there was no requirement for articles. For this reason, its members were more likely to come from less privileged families, and there was a higher proportion from overseas. It enabled its students to become qualified accountants without suffering a crushing financial burden.

Much has since changed. The profession is now more egalitarian, with the top accountancy firms vying to recruit the best candidates regardless of family background or wealth, and offering very attractive salaries and working conditions – too attractive, many believe. However, it must still sometimes seem odd to the general public to have members of two bodies providing the same services. This has become more so since the ACCA was granted its own Royal Charter, so that its members are now known as chartered certified accountants whilst the Institute's members are still designated as chartered accountants – all very confusing. There have been a number of proposals for a merger but they have been frustrated by the Institute's members' desire to guard jealously their perceived superior status. However, in 1955, the certified accountant route offered me a lifeline. Mr Morris was to employ me as an audit clerk at a reasonable salary, and I was to study in my own time at home to prepare for the examinations.

Mr Morris had a sole articled clerk, Malcolm Long, when I joined the firm – the East African student, who was to be the second, was not to arrive until sometime later. Malcolm was an alumnus of Stand Grammar School, which was near Radcliffe, and which was also the alma mater of Mr Morris and two other members of staff. It soon became clear that Malcolm's father had some concerns about the progress which his son was making. Malcolm and I worked together, side by side, doing the same work and enjoying the same conditions – except that I was being paid and he was not. Perhaps the father thought that his son should be working more closely with Mr Morris and should be receiving more personal supervision. But that was not how Mr Morris worked. Malcolm had also somehow established that the house in which I lived had no front garden, and that, therefore – he had worked out – the front door opened directly onto the street. A concept he found difficult to understand and a story which he had conveyed to his father. Little did he know that there was also no back garden. And if he had known that I was shortly to move to a council house in Woodhouse Park, I do not believe that he would have seen that as an improvement. Perhaps I was being over sensitive. In any event, his father arrived one day, at the office, to survey the scene. He was a travelling salesman, as they were called at that time, and he looked the part. I quickly formed the view, no doubt prejudiced, that he was a member of the petite bourgeoisie who was out to protect his minor privileges, and that he was ambitious for his boy. He went in to see Mr Morris. The outcome was that the articles were cancelled, a very unusual arrangement. Malcolm was to take articles with another chartered accountant in a larger, more prestigious firm – and one, perhaps, where his new colleagues were more likely to live in houses with front gardens. Money may well have changed hands because

J. Morris & Co. had been deprived of four more years of articled servitude. But Mr Morris was not happy.

The return to Woodhouse Park was to an enormous, sprawling housing estate which, in terms of house building, was now fully developed. It could no longer fairly be described as a desert without an oasis, but its amenities still left much to be desired. There was now a small parade of shops (which offered little more than the basic necessities), a Catholic church, and a public house where my father was soon to become known. There was no cinema, and no proper food shopping. A civic centre had long been promised, but would not be built for many years. The house, in Cotefield Road, was three-bedroomed, with a bathroom and separate lavatory (inside!), and a sizable garden. I had my own bedroom. My brother, Alan, was doing national service with the army at Windsor, where he was to meet his future wife, and then fall into the clutches of the Jehovah's Witnesses. He was not to return to Manchester. My father had developed a peripatetic life style, and it was never certain when he might turn up. He could be absent for several days, and then arrive, after a nightshift at work, as if he had never been away. Most of the time it was just my grandmother and me. My Auntie Kathleen had also moved to Woodhouse Park with her family and lived quite near-by, which provided company and comfort for Gran.

I was anxious to commence my studies in accountancy, but there was an initial hiccup when it was established that, because I had only four 'O' levels, it would be necessary to take a preliminary examination before I could be enrolled as a student member. This meant several months of preparation; and then I had to sit the examination without the outcome being at all certain. Fortunately, I got through without difficulty, but I certainly had my anxious moments. It was then, after much impatience, that I could start studies which were more relevant to my future career; as well as accountancy, company law, and taxation, the subjects to be studied included economics and business. The curriculum was wider than I had anticipated and this was to be helpful in broadening my horizons. I added other reading materials to the list of recommended books. These included *The Economist* magazine, at a time when its main story started on the outside front cover page. My grandmother would collect it from the shopping arcade newsagent, but for some reason she would ask for the 'Communist'. The assistant always gave her the correct magazine. They did not sell many copies of *The Economist* in Woodhouse Park.

I took a correspondence course with the Metropolitan College (for which, obviously, I had to pay, with money from my wages) and would regularly send in my papers, and look forward to their return with marks and comments. I worked at J. Morris & Co. for five and a half days each week (we still worked on Saturday mornings) and would return home on the bus from Piccadilly, the journey took one hour each way, for supper with my grandmother. I would then start work on my studies. For the first time, my life had a focus and a satisfying routine. The only break in this routine was the Saturday nights – although this was to become part of the routine in itself.

At Westmoreland Sanatorium I had become friends with Dick Maguire who lived in Chorlton-upon-Medlock, a poor part of Manchester between Victoria Park and the city centre. He had introduced me to several of his friends who were all parishioners of the Holy Name Catholic Church, where they were irregular attenders. We had taken to meeting on Saturday nights, usually at the College, a public house that was directly opposite the University of Manchester on Oxford Road. There might be six of us. We would establish ourselves at a corner table and stay there until closing time. We would each drink perhaps six or seven pints of bitter beer. I sometimes had difficulty walking from the pub, and often I would stay at the nearby home of one of the friends rather than returning to my own home. It might seem a joyless enterprise but it was not. It is difficult to explain and hard to justify, but we really did have a good time. I do not remember ever saying very much, and I suppose we did not really have very much in common. The others had all been brought up together, lived in the same streets, went to the same school, and attended the same church. I was still a bit of an outsider who had become friends because I had met Dick in hospital. But for me, it was the perfect release from the intensity and hard work of the week. Sometimes we would vary the routine and go to a dance at the Irish Club, which was in a neighbouring street, and where there would be Irish music and Irish songs and Irish dancing. Other times we would be interlopers at University dances, particularly for the Rag Day Ball; and we might visit the Holy Name Catholic men's club for snooker. But most Saturday nights we were at the College drinking seven pints of bitter beer.

The finances of J. Morris & Co. were often on a knife edge. Towards the end of the month, as the wages bill fell due, there would be hurried telephone calls to clients who might be persuaded to make a payment on account of an impending audit fee. There would then be discussions with the branch manager at Barclays Bank in Cross Street, where Mr Morris had introduced me so that I could open my own first proper bank account. I was only vaguely aware of these to-ings and fro-ings, but Mr Eastham, the cashier, would tell me that I should have no fear as Mr Morris would always sort things out. And he did. Mr Eastham would walk through the offices on pay day and give an envelope to each employee with the pay details. At Christmas time, on this errand, he took me to one side and said, in a whisper, that my pay this month included a bonus. He went on to say that I must not tell my colleagues. 'Mr Morris knows who does the work,' he said. That comment gave me almost as much pleasure as the extra money.

We dressed reasonably respectably and conservatively for the office. A tie was obligatory. But the shoes were not always highly polished, the suits sometimes shiny, and the shirt cuffs often frayed – but not the shirt collars. Also on Cross Street, opposite Barclays Bank, was a branch of Collars Ltd. Each week, I would take in my brown, stiff cardboard box, which they supplied, containing six soiled collars, and receive six clean collars in return. The collars were the property of the company, Collars Ltd., and I simply paid a laundering charge; an original and very convenient arrangement. The collars were white, came in three different styles, and were stiffly starched. The plain, white, collarless shirts were bought from Marks and Spencer, and, although there was a fresh collar each day, the shirts were often made to last two or even three days before laundering. That would not do today. A drawback of the heavily starched collars was that they were abrasive and chafed against the suit collar; the fabric could quickly wear away.

At the end of most days, Mr Morris would dash through the office with his customary rallying cry of 'Cum on now – quick's the word, and sharp's the action!' He would then disappear through the door to a waiting car which would take him to Victoria Station where, hopefully, he would catch the train for which he was already late. He often behaved in the manner of an old-fashioned Lancashire mill-owner; or even a Mississippi slave-owner. All he lacked was a whip. But there was always a smile lurking just beneath the surface. Or so I assumed. Another member of the audit staff was a Mrs Spencer who was the person who drove Mr Morris, in her own car, to the railway station, and to any out-of-office meetings. Each Thursday, they would go together to her home for lunch, which usually extended well into the afternoon. It is clear to me now, but was not at the time, that they were having an affair. I am not sure that I then knew what an affair was.

My father met Mr Morris for the first time on my twenty-first birthday. I had asked all my office colleagues to join me for a celebratory drink at a small bar which was in Rusholme, just beyond the point where Oxford Road became Wilmslow Road. I had first stumbled across the bar, literally perhaps, with my Holy Name friends, on a rare excursion after closing time at the College public house. It was primarily an after-hours bar at a time when the rigidly enforced licensing laws meant that public houses closed at half-past ten at night. My father arrived some time later than the rest of the group but he was soon locked in conversation with Mr Morris. He told me later that Mr Morris had said to him that he should not worry about me as he, Mr Morris, would look after me. My father took to Mr Morris, but he was not to have the opportunity to meet him again. I had bought myself a special birthday present. It was a watch with a gold casing which I purchased by mail order for 24 monthly payments of two pounds each. It was a lot of money. And it was on tick. I did not tell my grandmother.

I was walking from work, along Lower Mosely Street towards Piccadilly bus station, to catch the bus home to Woodhouse Park, when I heard about the plane crash in Munich. It was Thursday evening on 6 February 1958. Apparently, the crash had happened at three o'clock in the morning, but this was in the days before the 24 hours news cycle, and this news was only just coming through; certainly to the streets of Manchester. It was being said that the entire United team had been killed. An eerie silence seemed to settle on the city centre. People spoke in whispers, as they read the front page of the Manchester Evening News, and asked for the latest update. It was just too impossible to comprehend. The initial assessment turned out to be just a little pessimistic. But only a little... The full horror was that the heart had been torn from the side.

Eight had perished – as had many other passengers. Amongst the survivors were Matt Busby, the manager, and Duncan Edwards, the star defender; but both were seriously injured and in hospital. Matt Busby was to recover and would build another cup and league winning side. But Duncan Edwards, who was the finest footballer I was ever to see and who was still nowhere near his peak, did not. Several days later, a procession of hearses left Ringway Airport, and drove slowly down Princess Parkway. People lined the road. Grown men who had never cried in their lives, or at least not since childhood, stood bare headed, unashamedly awash with tears, and breathing heavily as if the oxygen had been sucked from the air. And silence. Just silence. Hardly a word was spoken. It was a long time before normal life was resumed in Manchester, and, for many, the memory remains fresh in the mind.

Professional footballers, at that time, were not well treated. The United team, and its management, were returning from their triumph, only hours before, in a European Cup tie. The supporters were still basking in its reflected glory when they heard the devastating news. The United entourage was rushing back to Manchester to meet the inflexible requirements of an intransigent Football League, whose management was not yet convinced of the merits of European football. A later return could have led to a deduction of valuable points from their football league challenge. It was this tight timetable which led to the risks which were taken in severe winter weather conditions, and, indirectly, to the tragedy. The maximum weekly wage for footballers – even the best – was £15. It was not much more than the average industrial wage. I was myself, as a modest audit clerk, earning nearly ten pounds a week. Today, a successful footballer's every whim is indulged, and he can earn more money in one week than the typical worker can earn in five years. How times have changed.

Immediately prior to my accountancy intermediate examination, I used one of my two weeks' annual holiday entitlement to stay at home for revision. I worked in the morning, had a sandwich for lunch, worked again in the afternoon, went for a walk in the now leafy streets of Woodhouse Park, stopped for a half-pint of beer at the only public house, and had supper with my grandmother. I did not shave. I had a new routine. Two months after sitting the examination, the result arrived in the post. I had passed and been placed third in the country in order of merit. Metropolitan College asked permission to use my name, as one of its more successful students, in the promotional material for its accountancy courses. Mr. Morris sent a telegram – I was at home with a mild ailment – to say well done, echoing the words of Brother Martin at the end of my first term at Xaverian College.

This time, I must not mess it up.

V
A POLITICAL ACTIVIST

My first recollection of anything remotely political was of the 1945 General Election. There was a polling booth at Birley Street school, and I remember standing outside and seeing and hearing Labour supporters singing 'Vote, vote, vote for Harry Thorneycroft, he is sure to win the day.' And he did. Labour won a landslide victory over the wartime leader Winston Churchill's Conservative Party. That first post-war Labour government went on to introduce the National Health Service and to start the nationalisation of basic industries and services; a programme of massive centralised government control which has, in health provision for example, and in other areas, still not yet been unpicked. In fact, it is possible to argue that government today is more heavily centralised than was the case then; we no longer have the strong city-based local government in places such as Birmingham, Liverpool and Manchester.

My grandmother, on every conceivable occasion, would respond to any unwelcome question with the refrain: 'Wait and see, as Asquith said.' But politics was rarely discussed at home. The family were Labour supporters, but I doubt that my father ever voted. For me, all that was to change in 1956, before I was even old enough to vote, with Suez.

At that time, I was living in a rented room in Victoria Park after a row with my grandmother. Angela, my favourite cousin from the reception desk at the Midland Hotel, had married Frank Ratcliffe. I was his best man. They were staying in the spare bedroom at Cotefield Road (my father must have been enjoying a longer than usual spell away from

74

'home') until they found a place of their own. Frank could be very argumentative, and, although this is not necessarily relevant to the story, he later turned out to be a fantasist and cross-dresser; he was a poor husband for Angela. He had a falling out with Gran for reasons which I cannot now remember. I sided with Frank, an act of total stupidity. Angela and Frank left the house. And, in a huff, and in an act of ungrateful solidarity, so did I.

The 'flat' in Victoria Park, again near Xaverian College – it seemed to act as some kind of magnet – was a single room in a decaying Victorian mansion. There was a gas ring on which I would prepare my evening meal, a metered gas fire, and a corner sink with hot and cold running water. A narrow bed, two chairs, and a small table completed the furnishings. A net-curtained window looked out to a central light-well. There was a shared lavatory and bathroom on the landing. I soon came across a neighbour, Alistair (Jock) Stewart, who rented an adjoining room. Jock spoke in a soft, refined (to my ears at least) Scottish accent – more Edinburgh than Glasgow – although he was not educated in Scotland but at Dulwich College in London. We became friends, and four years later he was to be the best man at my wedding. He was older than me, perhaps in his early thirties, and he was a counter clerk at the National Westminster Bank's principal Manchester branch in Spring Gardens.

I suppose that Jock had not made the progress he might have expected. He made it clear that he had no further ambitions. We took to discussing politics together late at night. He was a staunch supporter of the Conservative Party. My own views were probably not fully formed, although I was perhaps already developing a healthy scepticism of the ability of governments to change things. I would have been influenced by *The Economist* and by my now regular reading of the *Manchester Guardian*. Both were strong advocates of traditional liberal values, believed in free, open markets, and supported the United Nations and the upholding of international law. The *Manchester Guardian* had a radical and pioneering editor, Alistair Hetherington, and stayed close to its Manchester roots. Its philosophy could not have been more different from the statist, centralised, social democracy of the *Guardian* of today. The dropping of 'Manchester' from its masthead was much more significant than simply being a marketing ploy.

It was in the summer of that year that the Suez 'crisis', as it became known, began to dominate the front pages of our national newspapers. It became a deeply divisive issue in my late night talks with Jock Stewart.

The Egyptian leader, Colonel Nasser, had nationalised the Suez Canal in July 1956. Anglo-French forces invaded Egypt in October on the pretext of separating Egyptian and Israeli troops who were already in conflict. It later became clear, however, that there had been collusion between the British, French and Israelis, that the Israeli foray into the Sinai was a diversionary tactic, and that the real purpose of the invasion was to re-take the canal. There was worldwide condemnation, not least from the United States and the United Nations. It was in clear breach of international law. The whole enterprise became a fiasco, ending in ignominious withdrawal. It was deeply damaging to British interests. However, political passions were raised in a manner rarely seen before or since. Members of families were turned against each other.

My discussions with Jock Stewart didn't quite come to blows, but the language became increasingly heated.

In some quarters it was thought treasonable to question any aspect of the 'adventure'. The Labour Party initially supported Anthony Eden's Conservative government, but later relented. The Liberal Party stood out in unequivocal condemnation. The *Manchester Guardian* took a similar stance; the only national newspaper to do so. Its brave, lonely but honest stand was to cost it precious circulation. But it never faltered.

For me Suez was a catalyst. I now wanted to be involved in politics in some way to see if it really was possible to bring about change; and to find a better way of doing things. The idealism and innocence of youth. Jo Grimond had recently become the leader of the Liberal Party. He had succeeded Clement Davies, who, in 1945, at the Liberal Party's darkest hour, had taken over from Archibald Sinclair, the Liberal member of the coalition War Cabinet. Davies had not been able to improve the party's electoral fortunes, but he had at least held it together. Grimond was now articulating a Liberal philosophy in a refreshingly relevant style. I was in no doubt that it was to his party that I wished to offer my support.

There was no Liberal association in Woodhouse Park – I had returned to my grandmother's home – and I was directed to Withington Young Liberals, which was in one of the leafier suburbs of South Manchester. The branch chairman was Alan Share, who came from Sunderland where his family owned a large shop selling upholstered furniture, and who was a graduate of Oxford University. He was now a junior barrister in chambers which, conveniently, were in Princess Street, just next to the offices of J. Morris & Co. We were to become good friends. Alan soon involved me in political debates, about which he was a great enthusiast, but which for me was a new experience. I also quickly found that people prepared to take on responsibility are a rare breed, and I was promptly made an officer of the local association. A wider organisation of young Liberals in the North West was the Manchester Regional Young Liberals. Its chairman was Denis Wrigley, a charismatic, Methodist lay preacher (no, this is not an oxymoron), and a marketing executive with Turner and Newall. We were also to become life-long friends. Denis was a passionate orator, and he was never lost for an answer to any question, however obscure. He always seemed to have all the facts at his finger-tips. I was sometimes tempted to check on these 'facts', to see if they were quite as exact as he had suggested. But he always spoke with such conviction that he was never challenged. Denis, Alan, and I worked together as vocal and energetic activists, although, as well as being the youngest, I always considered myself the junior partner. We published several political pamphlets, and one of them, *Counterblast*, still has a resonance today. It sold 100,000 copies, at 1/6d. each, and was favourably reviewed by Bertrand Russell, although he did complain that we said too little about industrial policy.

The Liberal Party, at that time, had only six Members of Parliament, and registered only in the very low single figures of whatever opinion polls then existed. Two of the MPs – Donald Wade in Huddersfield East and Arthur Holt in Bolton West – were only elected as a result of pacts with the local Conservatives. The Conservatives agreed not to stand in one part of the town whilst the Liberals returned the compliment in the other part. The remaining MPs were confined to the outer fringes of the Kingdom. The Liberal revival under Jo Grimond's leadership was mainly evidenced, electorally, in the fevered atmosphere of by-elections.

Orpington, where Eric Lubbock triumphed, was followed by Mark Bonham Carter's success at Torrington. But it was difficult to hold by-election gains at general elections as the 'protest vote' became a 'wasted vote', under our first-past-the-post electoral system. Liberal fortunes ebbed and flowed between by-elections, but during the more than ten years in which I was an increasingly involved political activist, the number of MPs was never more than a handful, and the overall national support rarely got beyond the low single figure percentage. The important point, however, was that the Liberal fires were kept burning, and that a distinctive Liberal voice was heard in political discourse. Without Jo Grimond this might not have happened.

Manchester was one of the few places in the country where the Liberal Party boasted two full time, paid officials. Philip Robinson, in his Spring Gardens office, was the general secretary of the Manchester Liberal Association, and Neville Stanton performed the same role at the Cross Street offices of the North West Liberal Federation. Denis Wrigley and the rest of us thought, with youthful impatience, that they lacked sufficient energy. If something important needed to be done, it was to Denis to whom people turned. And he, increasingly, would involve Alan Share and me. Parliamentary by-elections, as I have mentioned already, were crucial in raising the party's profile, and putting Liberal views into the media. A by-election in nearby Rochdale took place in 1958. The Liberal candidate was the photogenic television presenter, Ludovic Kennedy. His wife was the ballerina and star of the film *The Red Shoes*, Moira Shearer. A perfect mix. Denis organised a cavalcade of support to leave Manchester for Rochdale on the crucial weekend before polling day. There was a convoy of more than 100 cars which converged on Rochdale on the Saturday morning. And it was very much Denis's convoy. He supervised every detail, bustling along from car to car making sure that the bunting was prominently displayed, and that each person was aware of his role.

Most of the supporters were to help with canvassing, but a small group of us were to stay in the Town Hall square, where a flat-backed lorry was to be the platform for an electoral hustings. Each of us was to speak in turn to keep the hustings going during what it was hoped would be a busy market day. I had not spoken before at a public meeting in the open air – and rarely indoors. I was nervous. I started speaking holding the microphone close to my face, but, after about 30 seconds, a colleague tapped me on the shoulder to say that the microphone was not switched on. I started again, and after a couple of minutes began to gain confidence. I remembered having been told that a useful oratorical trick was to engage a member of the audience by establishing eye-contact, and then to appear to be speaking directly to that person. I tried this, but my victim simply cleared his throat, spat in the gutter, and walked on. It was not a good start. Ludovic Kennedy did well in the by-election, but not quite well enough. We would need to regroup and prepare for the next time.

An interesting cameo from Rochdale was the prominent part played in the Labour campaign by Cyril Smith, who was then the Labour Mayor of Rochdale. He already had an unsavoury reputation, and there were many rumours about his private life. How the Liberal Party came to clutch him so close to its bosom after he left the Labour Party, and how David Steel came to recommend him for a knighthood, is beyond belief.

VI
BARBARA

I met Barbara in the Young Liberals in the spring of 1959. She had been recruited by Alan Share, although she was only mildly interested in politics. She was a vivacious, petite, dark-haired art student. Barbara was my first proper girlfriend. She lived with her parents and younger sister, Maria, in Longton Avenue, a tree-lined, cul-de-sac of semi-detached houses for the professional classes. Their immediate neighbours included a rabbi and a national newspaper editor. Barbara was born in the Charlottenburg suburb of Berlin in 1937. Her father had come to England at the beginning of 1939 to prepare the way for the subsequent arrival of his wife – it was the second marriage for both of them – and infant daughter. Barbara made the journey in her mother's arms in June 1939, with hardly any time left before a complete blockade stopped any further refugees entering Britain. The family settled in Manchester. Barbara's father had an older daughter from his first marriage, Annette, who had not been living with her father's new family, and who made her own independent journey, a little time after her father, as one of a party of children on the 'kinder transport'. All had been forced to flee for their lives from the evils of Hitler's democratically elected Nazi regime. Their experience made the religious intolerance with which I was familiar seem like the tiniest of pin-pricks.

The family name was Grunbaum, but this had recently been changed to Greenbaum, which seemed a half-hearted attempt at anglicisation – being neither one thing nor the other. Greentree or Greenwood might have seemed more

81

logical; but perhaps there was a desire not to be in total denial of their German, Jewish roots. For some strange reason, Barbara was not included in the name change – just her parents and younger sister (who had been born in Manchester in 1945) – but she was no longer a minor at the time, and she remained, until her marriage, Barbara Grunbaum.

Franz Greenbaum was a doctor of medicine, a psychiatrist, and an analytical psychologist. He had studied with Jung in Zurich, and was now one of the leading Jungian practitioners in England. His father, Max Grunbaum, Barbara's grandfather, was born in Budapest in Hungary and was an *haute couturier* tailor in Charlottenburg where some of his customers were the aspiring, impoverished artists of the period; German expressionists such as Zille and Otto Dix were amongst them. Sometimes, they might hope to pay their account with a rushed sketch; rather like Picasso, in his early days, with his restaurant bills. Dr Greenbaum – I cannot remember ever calling him Franz – was a consultant at two of Manchester's hospitals. The Home Office had given him permission to practice as a psychologist, but would not allow him to practise as a doctor of medicine. He also saw private patients in rooms at the home of a close family friend, Dr Alys Gregory, who was a senior lecturer in education at the University of Manchester. Dr Gregory lived in Palatine Road which was just two minutes' walk from Longton Avenue. It was here that he evolved, with some success, his own methods of group therapy. One of his patients was Alan Turing, of Bletchley Park fame, who, as well as receiving medical care, became a regular visitor at the Greenbaum family home, joining them for meals and family excursions.

Turing, a man of acknowledged scientific genius, cut a most unprepossessing figure. He had a heavy stammer, deeply bitten nails, and a bizarre dress sense. He was unkempt, and would be attired in a mismatch of eccentric clothes, at a time when people, generally, dressed conservatively. His gauche appearance ran counter to his desire not to draw attention to himself. After a homosexual affair with a younger man had been uncovered by the police, the courts had ordered that, as an alternative to prison, he be treated with the hormone, oestrogen, to reduce his libido. In the barbaric manner of those times, this was effectively chemical castration. Dr Greenbaum was trying to deal, amongst other issues, with the aftermath of this horror. Barbara was later to tell me of Alan Turing's last outing with her family. They went together to Blackpool, Turing wearing clothes which might have been better suited to the cricket field. He seemed happy and cheerful until he went to consult one of the many fortune tellers on the Blackpool promenade. When he left the booth, he was ashen-faced, and refused to discuss his experience. It seemed as if he had heard some dreadful premonition of impending disaster. He did not talk on the drive back to Manchester. They were not to see him again. Several weeks later he was found, dead. He had committed suicide.

Barbara's father was a man of obvious intelligence, great charm, warmth and presence; but he was also volatile, and had a short fuse. On what I believe was our only outing together – the whole family had been to the cinema – he exploded with rage, as he drove us back to the house (I was sitting in the back of the car with Barbara), as a result of a disagreement with his wife. He was to die on 1 November 1961, at the desperately early age of 58, as a result of a heart condition. He had always been a heavy smoker, and the stress of his life in Germany had taken its toll. He had also suffered the privations of being interned for several months in 1940, bizarrely, as an enemy alien, at Huyton in Liverpool. It was obviously a huge loss for Barbara, but it was also a blow for me as I would very much have liked to have known him better.

Barbara's mother was a dark, slim, elegant woman who retained her strong German accent throughout the whole of her life, and who was rarely seen without a cigarette in her hand. Hilde (always known as Hilla) Salinger was born in Schonlanke, then a town in the north east of Germany, but now in Poland under the new name of Trzianka. Her family owned and ran a significant fashion emporium and haberdashery. She met Franz Grunbaum, as he then was, in Berlin where they married. In Manchester, she suffered from agoraphobia, and was reluctant to leave the family home without her husband. After his death, when she was still in her forties, she made a full recovery, and was then to lead a normal life, although she did not re-marry. It was nearly two years before I was to call her by her first name, and she might have thought to have taken that initiative a little earlier. She was certainly a difficult woman, but eventually we had a good relationship, and I enjoyed spending time with her. She always stayed close to our family, and when we moved to London, she did too.

The Greenbaums led a quiet, modest, middle-class life in their three-bedroomed home; but it was certainly far better than anything I had so far come across. There were no obvious extravagances, apart from the long, family summer holiday, which was spent touring on the continent in the second luxury, Barbara's father's precious Humber Super-

Snipe motor car. They supported the Hallé Orchestra, visited the cinema, did not have television (few people did), rarely went to restaurants, and did not usually drink wine with lunch or dinner. Reading books was a favourite pastime. Religion played little part in their lives; they were not observant Jews, and Barbara was actually baptised in a Methodist chapel in Manchester. They had a wide range of friends from a variety of backgrounds.

Barbara had attended Whalley Range High School, and was studying textile design at the Manchester Regional College of Art when we met. Our first outing together was on a shopping expedition to Market Street, for a pair of shoes for Barbara. I am not one of life's natural shoppers, so I am unable to understand how I came to be coerced into such an enterprise. I would not recommend it for a first date. Soon, in what was not then the modern parlance, we were an 'item'. We would sometimes have supper together at one of the growing number of Indian and Pakistani restaurants, which were to become such a feature of Manchester's night-life in the future. On Sunday evenings we would usually eat at Barbara's home with her parents and sister. Dr Gregory, who was one of Dr Greenbaum's many admirers, but to whom he was often rudely sarcastic, would sometimes be there. The atmosphere could be tense, and the conversation, at least from my perspective, strained. Barbara's mother was a good cook, as is her elder daughter, but Sunday supper consisted of cold plates. There would be ham, salami and tongue from the continental delicatessen in Didsbury, and salads – which was not the usual fare at Cotefield Road. I would not take enough food onto my plate, perhaps feeling shy in unfamiliar surroundings, and would still be hungry at the end of the day.

Barbara did not fully share my enthusiasm for politics. At that time, few did. One Saturday there was a full-day Liberal Conference at the Methodist Hall in Manchester. Around lunchtime, Barbara again used her persuasive powers, this time to suggest our first visit to the cinema together. We went to the Odeon, which was nearby, where the film which was being shown was the new, gritty, fashionable *Room at the Top*. Based on John Braine's bestselling novel, it starred Lawrence Harvey, as a working-class boy with ambitions above his station.

Barbara had the use of Dr Gregory's Ford motor car for occasional excursions. She had passed her driving test at the first attempt at the age of 17. I remember one particular weekend when we drove together to Alderley Edge. I was wearing a new sports jacket and grey flannel trousers, which I had bought from Cecil Gee in Market Street. I was also wearing a cravat, which was new for me, and which I now think of as being slightly disreputable. But I felt very smart. We walked together along the 'Edge,' admiring the woods and the magnificent views, whilst I reflected on my life. I was still living in Woodhouse Park, still working at J. Morris & Co., but now spending much of my time on politics and with Barbara. And I must not forget that I still had to take my final accountancy examinations. Barbara wanted me to spend less time on politics and more with her, and that's what I wanted too. I felt happy and content. Everything seemed possible.

The Greenbaums' annual summer holiday was the highlight of their year. They would set out in the middle of July and return towards the end of August. Dr Greenbaum would drive his prized Humber Super-Snipe motor car, and they would travel through France, Germany, Switzerland

and Italy, stopping at roadside hotels on the way, visiting family friends at Basle, and – this year at least – spending two weeks at the seaside at Diano Marina in Italy. When Barbara left with her family in the summer of 1959, it was the first time we had parted since we had started to go out together. We agreed that we would stay in close touch, by post. I wrote every two to three days, and, in addressing the envelope would have to judge where she might be at the likely date of delivery. I would then wait, impatiently, and anxiously, for a reply. My letters followed Barbara around the Continent. Every letter had the same postscript: 'Please pass on my regards to Dr and Mrs Greenbaum and Maria.' Still very formal. The absence seemed to last forever, but, when she returned, I found, with enormous relief, that we still seemed to be happy with each other.

Before I met Barbara, I had bought a scooter – an NSU Prima. It was a stupid thing to have done because I could not even ride a bike. I quickly had two accidents, ruined a new suit, and spent some time being patched up in a doctor's surgery. Barbara persuaded me, she was getting rather good at that, to trade it in, and to buy a proper motor car. I bought a second-hand, 'sit-up and beg', black Ford Popular – on hire purchase. My grandmother's hold was weakening. In the autumn of 1959, we made an ambitious trip to London. Barbara had now graduated, and was seeking to continue her studies in Europe.

She had applied for a scholarship to the Leverhulme Trust, but had been told that she was ineligible, because she was not British-born. The Trust had very helpfully passed on her details to the Calouste Gulbenkian Foundation. The current Mr. Gulbenkian was known in the press as 'Mr. 5%', because of the enormous royalties he received on

Middle East oil revenues. Barbara was awaiting a response from the Foundation whilst she was on holiday, and I would ask in my letters: 'Any news from Mr. 5%?' When the news did arrive, it was of a very generous offer of a grant to study in continental textile centres. I sent a telegram to Barbara in Diano Marina: 'Heard last night (from Dr Gregory) the wonderful news from Mr. 5%.'

The scholarship was quite an achievement for Barbara, as the Foundation had not made grants of this nature before. Its secretary had suggested that Barbara, if visiting London, might call into their Regent's Park office, to discuss the format of the regular progress reports which they would require from her. It was the perfect excuse to spend a few days in the capital. We were to stay with my Aunt Miriam and Uncle André who had now moved from Ostend in Belgium to live in Streatham in South London. And my grandmother was to come with us. We went in my Ford Popular. Barbara had to do the driving as I had not yet passed my test. There were no motorways at that time, and we left Manchester on the A34 to begin our long, slow journey. We stopped off for lunch at Stratford-upon-Avon. We offered my grandmother fried scampi which she looked at suspiciously. It was a dish she had not seen before. She pushed the scampi around her plate, ate a few, and said she would not have them again. It was almost dark when we arrived in Streatham. My grandmother, sitting in the back of the car, had uttered hardly a single word.

Miriam and André had a restaurant and lived above it. André, perhaps because of his continental background, was disparaging about British food, and had pretensions for his new restaurant, where he was the chef-proprietor. However, it was closer to 'greasy-spoon', than Michelin star. But they

The only surviving photograph of my mother. It is at my Uncle John's wedding. She was already very ill, and is on the extreme left of the picture

With Alan and cousin Olive whilst still in short trousers

A hated photograph as an obnoxious goody-two-shoes, shortly after
my mother's death, with Alan, in our first long-trousered suits

The staff at J. Morris & Co. Mr Morris is the second from the left on the back row

My beloved grandmother on a visit to Sister Mary of St Cuthberger (my Auntie Betty). Miriam and Kathleen are also in the photograph

With Barbara on our wedding day

With Jo Grimond in Accrington at the 1964 general election

With Barbara at a Carborundum dinner party

The three boys at Diano Marina

terry
maher
liberal

Published by P. J. Handley, 78a High Street, Runcorn.
Printed by Garside & Mackie Ltd., The Guardian Press, Warrington

The front cover of the Runcorn election address in 1966

At No 10 Downing Street for a charity reception

With Barbara, and with Gordon Graham and his wife Friedel,
at a Booker Prize dinner at the Guildhall

Finishing off the cheese fondue after skiing

were welcoming, and hospitable, and Barbara and I were very happy staying with them. It was our first time away together. We went to a West End theatre to see the French musical *Irma la Douce*, and made the all-important visit to the Gulbenkian offices in Prince Albert Road, to finalise the details of Barbara's scholarship.

We were even able to fit in some politics. A general election had recently been announced, and I paid my first visit to the Liberal Party headquarters – then in Victoria Street – with copies of an election handbook, *Facts for the Fight*, which had been compiled and published by the Manchester Regional Young Liberals. I believe I went alone, Barbara, most likely, and certainly more sensibly, would have been in an art gallery. Later in the day, we went together to a Liberal election rally, at the Central Hall in Westminster, where the star performer was Jeremy Thorpe, who was soon to be elected as the Member of Parliament for Devon North.

On the return journey, from London, we made a detour to visit Barbara's half-sister, Annette, at Sandiacre in Derbyshire. She had recently married a prosperous Nottingham textile manufacturer, Rolf Noskwith, and she was busily organising their newly purchased first home. We had tea, and then resumed the drive back to Manchester, and to the election campaign. Barbara dropped me off first in Woodhouse Park, before returning to Withington, where my car was garaged at her family home. My grandmother had remained in London, and was to travel back by train later in the week.

I did not have a very distinguished role in the 1959 Liberal general election campaign. My main recollection is of manning the loudspeaker in the car which ferried Jo Grimond around Manchester on his whistle-stop tour, whilst manically repeating, 'Here is Jo Grimond, the leader of the Liberal Party'. It turned out, when the votes were counted, that the Liberals had made only modest progress; but the tone of the campaign had left the party's members in much better spirits. Harold Macmillan's Conservative Party was re-elected to form a new administration. Macmillan had become leader of the Conservative Party, and prime minister, after the short-lived premiership of Anthony Eden. Eden had been a successful foreign secretary, who had patiently waited for too long to succeed Winston Churchill as prime minister, and whose health and reputation had been ruined beyond repair by the Suez fiasco. Despite his success as housing minister in building 300,000 homes a year, his, 'You've never had it so good,' judgement of his own economic policy, and his 'Wind of Change' speech in South Africa, Macmillan was a disappointment. He was, I suppose, what would now be described as a compassionate conservative – but with decidedly patrician overtones. He seemed to have accepted the inevitability of a gentle downwards drift in terms of our influence in the world, and of our economic performance; and he had no ambition to roll back the state. Economically, he was more social democrat than liberal. It was not until Margaret Thatcher arrived on the scene that there was to be an alternative to this policy of simply managing decline. But that was still a long way ahead. And Wilson and Heath (and Home and Callaghan) were yet to come.

As I reached my twenty-fourth birthday, and with Christmas near, I began to have increasingly mixed feelings about Barbara's rapidly approaching move to Italy. She was to leave at the beginning of January. I had found it difficult to cope during the four-week summer holiday; this time she was to be away for a whole year. For Barbara it was the start of an exciting new chapter in her life. And perhaps, anyway, she would be glad to get away from my obsession with politics. Even New Year's Eve was spent together pushing leaflets through Woodhouse Park letter-boxes, with the message, 'Welcome to the Sixties, and a fresh approach from the Liberals'.

I had formed a new Liberal Association in Woodhouse Park, and had been persuaded by Philip Robinson to stand as a candidate at the next local election. Another commitment. As the day for Barbara's departure approached, my mixed feelings grew closer to panic. We had a number of serious talks together. Barbara's realistic view was that our relationship was still young and untested, and that there was a risk that it might not survive a year-long parting. 'You must not feel that you have to wait for me,' were almost her parting words, which was the last thing I wanted to hear. But we both pledged that, as in the summer, we would write to each other very regularly.

Barbara left on the third of January, staying overnight in Paris on her way to her studies in Rome. My first letter was posted on the following day, and they were then sent at regular intervals, whilst I waited feverishly for a reply. In the meantime, I threw myself even more energetically into Liberal Party politics. Within two weeks of Barbara's departure, I was adopted as the prospective parliamentary candidate for Accrington, and I write about my experiences there in a later chapter. I was already committed to stand in the Manchester council elections in May, and had much work to do as general secretary of the Manchester Regional Young Liberals. I was still earning my living at J. Morris & Co., and, of course, I had still to finish my accountancy examinations. There was little time to mope about Barbara, but nevertheless, I did.

One of my responsibilities in the regional Young Liberals was to organise weekend schools, which were held twice a year at Lyme Park in Cheshire. I had invited Francis Boyd, the political editor of the *Manchester Guardian*, to attend and speak at the 'school' which we had planned for the beginning of March. Boyd was the doyen of the political lobby at that time, and it was considered a coup to have secured him. He stayed for the whole weekend, was at the Saturday night party until the early hours, and made a thoughtful, encouraging, and flattering (to his hosts) speech. As part of our political activism, we sent a letter from Lyme Park to Hugh Gaitskell, the Labour Party leader, about some Labour Party internal squabble on nationalisation, the origins of which are now lost in the mists of time. It must have seemed important then, however, as it appeared on the front page of the following day's *Manchester Guardian*, under Francis Boyd's by-line. A few days later, he devoted the whole of his regular, weekly, and widely read column to his experiences at Lyme Park. He quoted extensively from a talk which I had given on housing – which was becoming my specialist subject – and particularly on housing conditions in Accrington. It could not have been a better thank-you letter.

Another way of keeping in touch with Barbara, apart from the letters (telephone communications hardly existed), was to visit her mother in Longton Avenue. This I would do on my way home from work. Hilla, which I had never yet called her, might be ironing, but she would stop, brew a pot of tea, and tell me whether her news of Barbara was more up-to-date than my own. We were slowly getting to know each other just a little better.

Barbara had been expressing some anxiety about her health in recent letters, and it all culminated, on the seventh of March, in an unprecedented telephone call to me from her mother. Barbara was pregnant. She had been able to overcome the practical problems of telephoning from Italy, it was neither convenient nor cheap, to deliver this devastating news to her mother. She was to fly immediately from Rome to London, where she would meet her parents at a flat in Chelsea, which was owned by her sister Annette and her husband Rolf. I was asked if I could travel to London to join them. It sounded like some awful family conference where my fate was about to be decided.

When I arrived in my taxi from Euston Station, Barbara was waving from a second-floor window; which helped to settle my nerves. It seemed a good omen. It was soon clear that we both wanted to be married to each other. And the sooner the better. It must have been the most enormous wrench for Barbara. It meant the abandonment of her studies, the return of the scholarship money, and the uncertain prospect of a very different kind of life. But she was firm; this is what she wanted. And I had not had a moment's hesitation. Before we went out to dinner, Barbara's mother – it was still Mrs. Greenbaum – had a private word with me. She reminded me that Barbara was a doctor's daughter, and she wondered whether I would be able to maintain her lifestyle. She was aware, of course, that I had not yet finished the examinations which would, hopefully, lead to my accountancy qualification. I sought to re-assure her, but had little doubt that she had harboured higher ambitions for her elder daughter. I was aware of the uncomfortable juxtaposition of my own position and immediate prospects with the obvious comforts of her step-daughter Annette's flat in one of the smartest parts of London. I spent the night of that momentous day in a nearby hotel, alone, and returned to Manchester the following morning to get back to work. Barbara remained in London with her parents to spend a day shopping for her trousseau, if that is not too grand a word to describe the modest purchases which were in contemplation.

The wedding took place at the Manchester Registry Office on the first of April. It seems extraordinary that things could have been arranged so quickly. It was a quiet, low-key event, with a wedding breakfast provided by Barbara's mother. The photographs were taken in the back-garden by Barbara's father. My best man was Jock Stewart, and the witnesses were Barbara's father and Dr Gregory. There were perhaps a dozen guests, including my father (he was wearing a pair of spectacles, one of the lenses of which was broken and held in place with sticking plaster, which for a man who took such great care over his appearance was strange; but he behaved well, and did not disgrace himself) and my Auntie Kathleen (my grandmother was not present as she felt that it would all be too much for her); Barbara's two sisters, Annette and Maria, and her brother-in-law, Rolf; and Barbara's aunt (her mother's sister) and uncle. My brother had been invited, but he was already committed to a Jehovah's Witness special retreat.

For a couple, intent on a quiet wedding, the first of April was not a good choice. Speculative press photographers were on hand to see which fool was marrying on April Fools' Day. They found one. A photograph appeared the following day in the *Manchester Evening News*. It was picked up by the *Accrington Observer* who, it would seem, were now monitoring my movements as one of Accrington's prospective parliamentary candidates. Its editor reprimanded me for my secrecy. 'You are now a public figure,' he said, 'and you can no longer behave as a private person.' I think that he was just a little bit over the top. The day after the wedding I was back at work. The honeymoon would have to wait for another year.

For the first four weeks of our married life, we lived in a large, one-roomed flat, with a corner kitchenette, and horrible, garish, pink-painted walls. It was in Palatine Road. However, we had been fortunate in quickly finding a house which we could buy, at the end of a short cul-de-sac in Lynway Drive, which was also in Withington, and which was only a ten minute walk from Barbara's family home. It was a 1930s three-bedroomed, semi-detached, brick-built house, with metal-framed, Crittall windows. It had a front and back garden. I was soon able to try my own hand at gardening, but it was limited to dahlias and sunflowers. That ambition did not last long, and Barbara very quickly became the family gardening expert. The house cost £2,250. I was able to secure a mortgage of £2,000 over 25 years at five and a half per cent interest. The balance of the purchase price, including expenses, was met by a loan from Alys Gregory – we were now on first name terms, although Barbara's mother was to remain Mrs. Greenbaum for several months longer, and her father was forever to be Dr Greenbaum. It was enormously generous of Alys, who was the Greenbaum's closest family friend, because the combined net worth of Barbara and me was zero, and, without that help, we could not have bought the house.

I still have a copy of our first household budget. My gross annual income from my employment was £750. It was the salary from a new job which I was meant to have started on the first of April, but which, of course, turned out to be our wedding day. I will write more about that later. After tax and national insurance, the net income became the equivalent of £12 and 10 shillings each week. We had agreed to take in a lodger, until our finances improved, to occupy one of the spare bedrooms, and this would bring in an additional £2 a week. In total we had £14 and 10 shillings, to cover weekly expenses. The mortgage payments were £3, £5 was allowed for housekeeping, £1 was assumed for the repayment of Alys's loan (although, in a further act of kindness, she had said that this could be deferred), £1 was for heating and lighting, 15 shillings for rates, 10 shillings for the telephone, 10 shillings for laundry, and £1 for my lunches and bus fares – the Ford Popular had been sold as part of the belt-tightening. It amounted to a total of £12 and 15 shillings. There was little margin for error. The whole enterprise was dependant on the rental income from the lodger; and a baby was on the way. But, within two months of receiving that fateful telephone call from Barbara's mother, we were married, and we had our first home. It was ours. At least subject to the mortgage, and Alys's loan.

VII
A PARLIAMENTARY CANDIDATE

I must have been the first prospective parliamentary candidate of any party to have been adopted after the 1959 general election; and, as this happened just one month after my twenty-fourth birthday, I was, for quite some time, the youngest. I had been asked to address a meeting of Accrington Young Liberals sometime before Christmas. Shortly afterwards, I saw Neville Stanton, the secretary of the North West Liberal Federation, at the Reform Club, in Manchester's King Street. I was a new member of the club, where I had recently taken to having lunch. It was conveniently close to my office at J. Morris & Co., had strong traditional Liberal connections, and had once had Lowry as a member. Many of our political committee meetings were now held there. Neville told me that Accrington Liberals had been in touch with him and that they wanted me to be their candidate at the next general election. As the last general election had only recently been held, this was clearly a long way off. At that time, there was no central list of approved candidates. Neville was effectively the king-maker in the North West, and he very quickly gave me his backing. But he reminded me of the long list of my existing commitments. I easily convinced myself that if I was serious in wanting to promote liberal ideas and policies, then I must stand as a candidate for parliament, and that Accrington was a good opportunity. It seems a little naïve and unrealistically optimistic now, but that is what I agreed to do.

Accrington had not had a Liberal parliamentary candidate for more than 50 years; since the general election of 1908. To describe the local Liberal Party as a 'skeleton organisation' would have been an exaggeration of its strength. It hardly existed at all; and it had very little money. Its active members were mainly the Young Liberals, and most of these were from the sixth form of Accrington Grammar School. They, together with several of the school's teachers, including its headmaster, were all party members and had been the driving force in seeking a parliamentary candidate. They had wanted to do this at the earliest possible moment, because they realised just how much work would need to be done.

There were two, nominally, Liberal members of Accrington Town Council, but they were there solely as a result of a pact with the Tories, and were now apprehensive about the possible impact that a Liberal parliamentary candidate might have on their cosy arrangement. They were Liberals in name only, and could not be relied upon in building for the future; in fact they were an obstruction. As they say in those parts, 'they would go anyway for a pint'. One of the councillors was also the secretary of Accrington Stanley Football Club, and was known to send out postcards, through the open mail, without envelope, headed 'private and confidential'. I actually received one. Accrington Stanley's problems were not confined to the football pitch.

To have any chance of success, we would need to build a ward organisation, fight local elections, and establish a fund to finance the general election campaign. I had made it clear at the adoption meeting that I would not be able to devote the time which this would require until later in the year, when some of the existing demands on my time might have been reduced. At the very least, I must finish my accountancy examinations.

In May, I fulfilled the ill-advised promise to stand as a candidate for Woodhouse Park in the Manchester council elections. The campaign was little more than a one-man band, although we did make quite a lot of noise in the local newspapers. It had all come along a little too quickly. I really had taken on too much. We came a poor third, which was, I suppose, par for the course, at that time. At the count, at Manchester Town Hall, the presiding officer was Leslie Lever, who was then the Lord Mayor of Manchester, as well as being the Labour Member of Parliament for Ardwick. His brother, Harold Lever, was also a Member of Parliament for another Manchester constituency, and was to become chief secretary to the Treasury in Harold Wilson's Labour government. Leslie Lever was a prominent member of the Jewish community, but he was also close to the Catholic hierarchy. Astonishingly, at the annual Catholic Whit walks, he would be seen at the side of the Bishop of Salford, leading the procession. He was appointed, by the Pope, as a Knight Commander of the Order of St. Gregory the Great, an honour previously unheard of for a non-Catholic. As the counting of the votes got under way, Leslie took me to one side to ask for which party I was standing. When I told him, he said that he was really a liberal at heart. It seemed as if his politics might be as interchangeable as his religion. Or perhaps he was just a very good politician.

Another example of over-commitment came about as a result of my election to serve on the committee of the National League of Young Liberals. On a rare visit to London, I attended my first meeting, at the National Liberal Club, still harbouring a deep, and natural, suspicion of southerners. Real people, and real politics, I thought were in the north – and that meant mainly in Lancashire. I remember a discussion over a sandwich lunch. Somebody was describing an experience whilst canvassing in a recent election in Kensington. Apparently, an elector, when confronted on the doorstep, had said with some passion, that she would not vote for the Conservative candidate because he split his infinitives. I was not entirely sure what a split infinitive might be; it was not a subject often raised on the doorsteps of Manchester and Accrington. Nevertheless, I have since been careful not to split my own infinitives. Just in case. But it did little to dispel my opinion of those who lived in the south.

It was the autumn of 1960 before I was able to spend a serious amount of time in Accrington. I was by then no longer involved in local politics in Manchester, was settled in our home in Withington, and had passed my final accountancy examinations. I was now a qualified accountant. I was still involved in the regional Young Liberals, and our first son, Nicholas, had arrived in September; but for the next four years I was to spend three nights each week, after work, and occasional weekends, canvassing and campaigning in Accrington. It involved a journey of a little more than an hour each way, usually by car, but sometimes by train. They were long days.

Accrington was predominantly a working-class area. It was represented by a Labour Member of Parliament, Harry Hynd, but had a surprisingly resilient Conservative vote. Apart from the main town, the constituency included the satellite villages of Oswaldtwistle, Clayton-le-Moors, Church and Rishton. Each had its own identity and local council – and cricket team; Lancashire League cricket was, and remains, a very important part of local life. There was no Liberal representation in any of these outlying areas, and one of our main tasks was to establish local Liberal associations, and to find candidates to stand in the council elections. Parliamentary candidates would not now be expected to undertake these activities, but we really were starting from scratch. There was no alternative.

There was a sound industrial base in Accrington. The cotton mills were no longer important, but engineering, including the manufacture of textile machinery, was strong, and there was also coal mining. One of the consequences of this was the proliferation of working men's clubs, including miners' clubs. There must have been around 50 within the constituency, most of which I succeeded in visiting before the general election.

The town had suffered more than its fair share of grief. At the start of the First World War, Accrington had formed one of the earliest of the 'pals' regiments, where neighbours and factory friends – often whole families – had ganged-up together to line up in front of the recruiting sergeant and volunteer to fight for their King and Country. A whole generation of young working men had marched cheerfully away, singing patriotic songs, to almost certain death.

Another feature of Accrington was the strength and importance of its local newspaper, the *Accrington Observer*. It made quite a splash at the arrival of the first Liberal parliamentary candidate for 50 years, and was always anxious for copy. I made sure that it was kept well supplied. Whatever I fed to the friendly reporter would appear in print in its next issue. I would deliver a copy of a speech which might have been made to no more than a couple of fellow Liberals, but it would find its way into the newspaper. It gave the appearance of great activity. I had an early meeting with the editor. Harry Hynd had a regular column bringing 'News from Westminster'. I suggested that I should be allowed equal space to write my own weekly article. He readily agreed, and for the next few years, at two o'clock each Sunday afternoon, I could be found, at home, sitting in front of my typewriter, with the need to write 800 words on a subject often still to be decided. It had to be finished in time to meet the four o'clock deadline of the Sunday post. Today, candidates of all parties are spoon-fed with briefings and lines-to-take, on a daily basis, by headquarters-based researchers and other policy geeks. Articles are often written for them. But, at that time, there were no communications from above; I was hardly aware of a party central office. I was on my own. I must often probably have been out of my depth, although, of course, I didn't realise it at the time. One rarely does.

One issue which I made very much my own in campaigning in Accrington was housing. There were still areas in the centre of the town where families were living in back-to-back homes, and having to share lavatory facilities in communal privies. My grandmother had always insisted – correctly – that we had never lived in slum conditions. But these Accrington ghettoes were truly slums of the worst possible kind. They made Viaduct Street seem like Claridge's. I sought to apply pressure on the local council to accelerate its house building programme. Nationally, the target of building 300,000 houses a year was close to being achieved, and, of these, half were council houses. Accrington was dragging its feet. I was able to raise the subject at the annual Party Conference which was held at Llandudno, in North Wales. At the end of my speech, I was surrounded by a small posse of press photographers, and the following day the story was featured on the front page of the *Manchester Guardian*, together with a photograph. Fame at last; and embarrassment for the Labour-controlled Accrington Town

Council. The housing challenge at that time was to re-house families who were living in appalling conditions; and that challenge was largely met. Today's challenge is to add to the total housing stock to cope with the significant increase in the size of the population – mainly from immigration, and the higher birth-rate of immigrant families – and the response has been lamentable. There is still no sign of any real sense of urgency.

The general election was held in October 1964. The Conservatives had to change their candidate rather late in the day, as the long-standing candidate's health had deteriorated. He was replaced by Victor Montagu, who had formerly been the Earl of Sandwich, and who was married to a daughter of the Duke of Devonshire – a sister of the wife of Harold Macmillan. It was later alleged that he had failed to consummate the marriage, and it was dissolved. His introduction to Accrington was facilitated by legislation which had recently been passed as a result of a campaign led by Tony Benn, formerly Viscount Stansgate, and which enabled Montagu to renounce his title, and therefore to be eligible to stand for election to the House of Commons. I was able to make play on the contrast between Mr Montagu's privileged background and the privations of many of his constituents. On hearing of his adoption, I referred to him as an 'aristocratic anachronism'. Hardly the neatest turn of phrase, but it was to appear on the front pages of a number of national newspapers.

I used my two-week holiday entitlement from work to concentrate on the final stages of the election campaign. Barbara joined me for the second week. We now had three small boys. Barbara's mother looked after the oldest, Nicholas, and the youngest (he was only nine months old), Jeremy, whilst the middle one, Anthony, came with Barbara and me to Accrington. We stayed in the home of my unpaid election agent, and Anthony went to a nearby nursery school, where he was not very happy. We would usually have fish and chips in the middle of the day, and a sandwich in the evening, whilst we pounded the streets of the town and its surrounds, and I addressed factory gate meetings at morning, noon, and night. There was a growing Pakistani community in the town, and we printed an election leaflet in Urdu which we handed out on market days. It would now be commonplace, but was not so at the time. Granada had just started television broadcasts for all of the candidates in its area. When Accrington's turn came along, each of its three candidates made a short prepared speech, and it was thought by the local press that I did well. Election meetings were well attended, and we had a good reception on the doorstep. We were becoming just a little optimistic. Accrington Grammar School held a 'mock' election, and the Liberal candidate came first. This was reported in the local newspapers, as was news of the now narrowing odds which local bookmakers were offering on a Liberal victory in Accrington. We had a packed eve-of-poll rally at Accrington Town Hall – those are now really far-off days – addressed by Arthur Holt, the Liberal Member of Parliament for Bolton West, and myself.

It is incredible, how normally rational people, pursuing the most hopeless of lost causes, can convince themselves that they might just be about to win. Which was the trap we fell into. The opposition, we were again told by the press, were getting a bit rattled. They need not have been. We polled respectably, saved our deposit (the threshold then was 12.5 per cent, whereas today it is only five per cent), which was an achievement for a Liberal candidate at that time, particularly in a constituency which we had not contested for more than 50 years. But we were a poor third. My election address had stressed local issues, including, once again, housing. I advocated the use of new building materials and factory-produced system building techniques to deal more swiftly with the legacy of so many homes which were still without a bath, inside lavatory and running hot water. The election however had been decided on national issues, mainly the economy. As so often happened, the Liberal vote had been squeezed. Labour had campaigned against the '13 wasted years' of Conservative government, and its leader, Harold Wilson, had spoken of 'the white heat of the technological revolution.' The only recently appointed, and now about to be deposed, Conservative prime minister. Sir Alec Douglas-Home, who had succeeded Harold Macmillan, had sought to defend his party's record, but had been ridiculed for his 'matchsticks' economics. Labour won, but with an overall majority of only four (Douglas-Home had fared better than predicted) and within two years there would be the need for a further general election.

I fought the subsequent election, in the spring of 1966, as the Liberal candidate for Runcorn. Accrington did not have the financial, emotional, or organisational resources to contest another election so quickly; and it was thought that Runcorn offered better prospects. It had an established organisation, was reasonably well funded, had achieved some recent success in local elections, and had an experienced election agent. This time, unlike Accrington, the selection of a candidate was much more professional. I was on a short-list of three, and we all arrived, at the same time, to address, separately, the executive committee of the local party. The other two hopefuls were also active and enthusiastic Young Liberals who I knew well, one a schoolteacher, and the other a local government officer. We waited together, with a slight air of embarrassment, for the verdict to be announced. I was the 'lucky' one. I now had to get to work immediately to prepare for an election, the date of which had not yet been set, but which could not be long in coming. I had less time to establish myself than at Accrington, and there was, therefore, a greater sense of urgency; but I had much more help and support.

The town of Runcorn was the hub, but the constituency stretched into the more prosperous parts of Cheshire, as far as Frodsham. The main local employer was ICI, where the jobs were better paid and more highly skilled than at Accrington. It felt middle-class, comfortable, and settled. It was more garden parties and church fetes, than pit-heads and factory-gates. A safe Conservative seat.

Runcorn, indirectly, led to my first appearance in a court of law. I had arranged to buy a new motor car, a Triumph Herald, which I would be using in the election campaign. The purchase got off to a bad start. My drive home from work took me past the showroom window of the motor car dealer. In traffic, I looked sideways, to sneak an admiring glance at my new car. I ran into the car in front. Sheepishly, I went into the garage to explain that the car which they had agreed to take in part-exchange for the new car was now in the road outside, incapacitated. They were understanding. But my woes did not end there.

Whilst speaking on a hand microphone from my shiny new car, in Runcorn Town Centre, the front off-side passenger door swung free of its attachment and hit and dented the bodywork. After the election, I took the car back to the garage for repairs. When I later went to collect it, I was presented with a bill and told that I could not have the car until it was settled. I repeated the claim, which I had made earlier, that the door had not been properly secured on delivery, and that, therefore, it was their responsibility. To no avail. Then, in a fit of pique, I jumped, perhaps in retrospect unwisely, into the car, found that the key was in the ignition, and drove away as the shouts and curses faded into the background. Some months later, when I had assumed that the matter had gone away, I received a writ. I consulted the company secretary of my employer, who was a solicitor. He said that the best policy would be for me to appear in person before the judge, without a lawyer, and to tell him, in my own words, what had happened. He thought that the judge might be sympathetic if I was seen to be representing myself. It was good advice. The fierce-looking garage owner sat, with his legal team, on the opposite side of the court, glowering at me, as I told my story. The judge found in my favour. My angry adversary, from whom I had been in fear for my life, came across, smiled, and shook hands.

We fought a more professional campaign in Runcorn, with much better resources, and we polled well. But I had preferred Accrington and its working men's clubs. We again finished third, behind the successful Conservative candidate, Mark Carlisle, who would later be the education minister in Ted Heath's government. For the moment, however, Harold Wilson and Labour were still in power, and this time with a comfortable, working majority. It was to be many years before I was again involved actively in the Liberal Party. Politics was to take a back seat as I concentrated on my business career and the needs of a growing family. I was 30 years of age.

VIII
A BUSINESS LIFE

1. The Co-operative Wholesale Society

I left J. Morris & Co. on 31 March 1960, the day before my wedding. I had been there for more than five years. After the results of my intermediate examination in 1958, I had finally been earning a salary which was similar to the wages which my Holy Name friends, who were all skilled trades- men, had been receiving for some years. Mr. Morris paid, I suppose, the market rate – he would certainly not have wanted to pay more – and I would have been paid at least as much as colleagues of similar experience. A particular col- league, Maurice Hartley, became a friend, and, in discussing ambition, he would define it in financial terms. 'I suppose,' he would say, 'should we get to earn £1,000 a year, we will have done well.' Poor Maurice was never to achieve his am- bition. He was another alumnus of Stand Grammar School, and he collapsed and died when refereeing a rugby football match at the school playing fields. He was 34 years old.

If I was to achieve my own ambitions, I would, of course, first have to take my final examinations. It might have been more sensible to have stayed with J. Morris & Co. until after that event, when I could then have sought new employment as a qualified accountant. I had already formed the view that I would not want to stay in a small accountancy practice, but to broaden my experience in some larger enterprise, and then see how things developed. It was with this in mind, and also with the hope of increasing my earnings, that, at the beginning of 1960, I started to look for new job opportunities. Little did I then know that I would soon have the additional responsibility of a new family.

In any event, in February, I responded to an advertisement in the *Manchester Guardian* – where else – for a job with a firm of accountants, which was described as the 'official auditors' of the Co-operative Wholesale Society (the CWS). The CWS was one of the biggest business organisations in the country. It has recently been somewhat diminished, but is still of great size. It embraced the Co-operative Insurance Society, the Co-operative Bank, a national chain of chemist's shops, and numerous plantations and manufacturing installations overseas, apart from its principal activity as the wholesale supplier of the requirements of the regional retail societies – the high street presence through which the Co-operative movement was best known to the general public.

This enormous enterprise was audited by a group of just eight people – four principals and four assistants – and I was offered a position as one of the assistants. It was a very odd arrangement. Technically I was to be employed and paid by the CWS, but, in practise, I worked for one of the four principals, to whom I reported. The principals, the official auditors, had their own letter-heading and practice name to suggest an independent firm, which it was not. It seems to me now to have been a necessary charade to satisfy the requirements of the regulatory authorities; an example of the eccentric methods of corporate governance at the CWS with which we have all recently become familiar. The auditors had a single client, the CWS, and they were appointed, individually, by election, through the votes – for which they must canvass – of the powerful retail societies, who were the shareholders and effective owners of the CWS. They were paid a fixed salary and expenses by the

CWS. They were its employees, not independent auditors. This arrangement was abandoned, much, much later, and the 'official auditors' were subsumed into the international accountancy firm KPMG.

The principal to whom I reported, Mr Gibson, was the 'senior partner,' although, as I have tried to explain, it was not really a partnership. Mr Gibson was a man in his fifties who looked the part of a successful, prosperous professional, which he most certainly was. He was grey-haired, softly spoken, well-mannered, and wore well-tailored suits and highly polished shoes. Very much 'old school'. He lived in one of the plusher parts of Cheshire, from where he would be driven to his office each day in his chauffeur-driven, expensive motor car. As I was to discover, it was one of the many perks of this unusual arrangement. I was later to benefit from this, as, whilst I was waiting for my bus on Wilmslow Road, his car would sometimes pull up by the bus stop, and he would ask me to join him in his privileged ride to work.

Mr Gibson offered me a salary of £750 per annum (this was the income on which our first household budget was based), for a probationary period, after which, he said it could be substantially increased. He expected me to complete my examinations as soon as possible. As I wrote to Barbara at the time (she was still at the British School in Rome), the new job should vastly increase my experience, and would involve some travel, including a stay in London for six separate weeks of the year. I said that I envisaged it lasting for perhaps two years, after which I would look to move into industry – which is roughly what happened.

The meeting with Mr Morris, at the end of February, when I told him that I wished to leave, was uncomfortable.

He clearly felt that I was being disloyal. He had given me my start in life, and had assumed that I would qualify whilst working in his practice, and make my career with him. He was disappointed, and there was no warmth in our parting. As I mentioned in an earlier chapter, it was to be 30 years before I was to see him again, at the funeral of a mutual friend. We were not then able to establish any kind of dialogue at a serious level, but he was cheerful, and jokey, telling anybody who would listen that he had taught me everything I knew. It was the old Mr Morris, and I was very happy to see him. And he was still 'Mr Morris'.

I was due to start my new job on 1 April 1960, but, of course, the process had been overtaken by events, and this was now to be my wedding day. I, therefore, started a day later. I met Mr Gibson at the beginning of the day and told him that I was now a married man. He was somewhat disconcerted. In making the appointment, he had assumed that, as a single person, I would not be inconvenienced by the travel arrangements, which were a necessary part of the job. He said that he would not feel comfortable in sending a newly married man to London for six weeks each year, as well as visits to other parts of the country involving overnight stays. He would need to re-allocate responsibilities, and get my new colleagues to take on some of my travelling assignments. I would spend more time at the head office in Balloon Street. It was an unwelcome inconvenience for him, but he was as good as his word.

I did go out on distant audits from time to time, but mostly I was in Manchester, often auditing the affairs of the Co-operative Insurance Society. This was not the most exciting project, although I would sometimes allow myself to be diverted into spending more time than was justified in examining a file of some complex and absorbing insurance claim, where I had to ensure that proper provision had been made for any likely liability. The occasional visits to subsidiary businesses, and to the London head office in Leman Street, were a welcome change from the Manchester routine. They were also a useful source of additional income. The travelling allowances were extremely generous. My weekly pay would be boosted with the proceeds of my expenses claim – everybody who worked at the Co-op was paid weekly – and it was easy to see why my colleagues had been willing to share my part of the travelling burden, in addition to their own.

My first trip away from home was to Tonbridge, in Kent, where we were to audit a company producing cricket bats and balls, and other cricketing paraphernalia. It was one of a hotchpotch of businesses, owned by the Co-op, which had been acquired over the years, without, it would seem, any clear strategy or obvious connection to the ideals of the Co-operative movement's founding fathers in Rochdale. We stayed at an idyllic inn in the centre of the town, and, whilst Barbara was moving into our new home in Withington, I could be found, in the early evening's spring sunshine and in bucolic surroundings, with a pint of beer in my hand. Barbara would often remind me that I always seemed to be away from home when we were moving house.

My next out-of-town audit was in August, and involved a week's work in London at the Co-op's Leman Street offices. I was returning to Manchester from Euston Station, on the Friday afternoon, when, whilst walking along the train corridor to find a suitable place to settle, I was surprised to see Barbara's parents sitting together in one of the first class compartments. First class was not their normal mode of travel, but, whilst in London, I had heard from Barbara that her father had suffered a heart attack in the South of France, when on their usual summer holiday. He had been advised by his doctor to leave the Humber Super-Snipe in France, and to return home by plane and train. They insisted that I join them in their compartment, paying for the up-grade when the ticket inspector came along. We were still on fairly formal terms, and Dr Greenbaum was pale and tired, all of which led to a long and awkward journey. He had been a life-long chain smoker – as was his wife – but he had stopped immediately after the heart attack, and he now devoured an endless supply of peppermints. It was to be of no avail, and he was to die in a little over a year's time.

Barbara and I had our first holiday together a year after our wedding, as her mother looked after Nicholas, who had arrived in the previous September. It was in the nature of a delayed honeymoon. We went for a week to Paris, and stayed in a small hotel on the left bank, in an area which, some months earlier, had been the scene of student riots. The best that could be said about the hotel was that it was clean and cheap. It was at a time of exchange controls, the limit was £50 per person, and the newspapers would suggest ways in which it was possible to enjoy a European holiday, whilst staying within the limits; not that the controls were of any concern to us, as we would not, in any event, have been able to afford to spend more. One of the newspaper articles was 'How to live in Paris on £5 a Day', and this became our bible. Choosing from the suggestions in the article, we were able to eat out each day, very well, whilst staying within our tight budget. I can still taste the crêpes.

Each year, two of the principals would visit the overseas possessions of the CWS, many of them on the sub-continent, and this brought, as a reward, one of the most valuable of their many perks. They would be kitted out, at the expense of the CWS, with every conceivable item of clothing, and other accoutrement, which might be needed in the tropics, and any other far-flung parts which they might visit. And they would usually have three of each. The principals alternated on these excursions, and, therefore, every two years, the exercise would be repeated. They must have had very large wardrobes.

It was in the middle of my second year at the CWS, when Mr. Gibson must have been on one of these jaunts, that I had a long talk with one of the other principals. He said that he and his colleagues could see that I was ambitious, but that the only possible progress I could make was to become a principal myself. Should a vacancy arise, this would involve currying favour with the delegates from the retail societies who voted, at their annual meeting, to select the individual official auditors. The Co-operative movement supported the Labour Party and sponsored many Labour MPs, and the delegates were often Labour Party activists. I was a member of the Liberal Party, and a prospective parliamentary candidate. It would be impossible for me to express the Labour sympathies which a successful bid to become an official auditor would require. The principals, he said, were very happy for me to continue with my present duties, for as long as I wished, but he would be surprised if this would satisfy me for very long.

It was an accurate assessment. The job was a dead-end; and the routine of the work was repetitive and boring. Much of it was in the nature of an internal audit, rather than the arms-length, objective scrutiny of the accounts which you would expect from an independent firm of accountants.

Since the arrival of our first son, Nicholas, I had been mainly head-office based, without any travelling, which meant that the work did not have the variety which I had at first envisaged. It lacked the range of activities which I had enjoyed at J. Morris & Co., and, in the event, it had done little to broaden my experience. But I was now qualified as an accountant, and, perhaps, I had gained a little more in self-confidence. Barbara assumed the role of looking each day in the jobs pages of the *Manchester Guardian*.

2. Private Practice

Whilst I was earning a living from the day job, and spending much of my time on politics, I also developed a parallel activity, which was to become a very useful side-line.

One of the oddities of the times of which I am now writing, 1950s and 60s, was that an accountant, unlike, for example, a solicitor, was able to offer his services to prospective customers without having passed any examinations. It was not unusual, when walking along the streets of the central business area of Manchester, to see a brass plate on an office door, with a name, followed by the word 'Accountant', without any suggestion of any formal qualifications. Under the Companies Acts, he would not be able to sign the balance sheet of a limited company, but there were few other restrictions, so, for example, he would be able to offer advice to, and prepare accounts for, sole traders and partnerships, and prepare tax returns for individual clients. This was to create an opportunity for a new source of income for me, before I had completed my own examinations, although it happened entirely by chance.

It must have been towards the end of 1958, before I

had met Barbara, and at a time when I was spending more time with the Liberal Party and less with my Holy Name friends, that I found myself, late on a Saturday night, at an impromptu party at the Stockport home of Vic Child. I had not met Vic before, and I cannot now remember how I came to be at the party, but he must have heard that I was an accountant, of sorts, and he told me that he had a tax problem, and that he would like to discuss it with me.

It turned out that he had been working as a self-employed building contractor for the past three years, and that the Inland Revenue were pursuing him for a tax bill of more than £1,000; which, at that time, was a large sum of money. Vic was personable, and persuasive, but also rather helpless. I agreed to try to help him. In the absence of any tax returns or trading accounts, and in the light of his failure to respond to any of their numerous letters, the Inland Revenue had raised what were described as 'estimated assessments'. It was from these that the tax liability had been calculated. So, as a half-qualified accountant, still short of his twenty-third birthday, I rang the tax office to see what could be done. I had to leave the offices of J. Morris & Co. to make the call from a public telephone, as this was not practice business, and I did not yet have a telephone at home. I spoke to the appropriate Inspector of Taxes. I explained that I had been asked to act for Mr Child; that Mr Child's strengths were not in administration; that I had now been asked to prepare accounts for him; and that I would ensure that his tax affairs were dealt with in a timely manner in the future.

The key question, which I had to put to the Inspector, was to ask if he would accept a late appeal against the estimated assessments, as the time allowed for appeals had long since expired. He agreed, without any hesitation, subject only to the condition that accounts were to be submitted to him within the next four weeks. I spent my next two weekends preparing Vic's trading accounts from his very incomplete records. The tax liability was ultimately settled at less than £100, a large reduction from the originally assessed figure of more than £1,000. A much relieved Vic Child was more than content to settle my fee note of 15 guineas; I had continued the professional tradition of raising bills in guineas, which in retrospect now seems a rather silly affectation. In any event, whether in pounds or guineas, the sum was the equivalent of more than one week of my salary from J. Morris & Co. In all my dealings with the staff at local offices of the Inland Revenue, I found them to be entirely helpful if there was an honest, straightforward presentation of the facts (no waffle), and that if promises, once made, were kept. It seemed to me, that they shared a desire to resolve problems, rather than seeking to exploit a vulnerable tax-payer.

Vic Child was my first client. But word soon got around the Stockport building trade that I was open for business. Several of Vic's acquaintances became clients. Principal amongst them was George Davis, a genial, though foul-mouthed (for some reason, rarely in my presence, and never in his own home), Glaswegian plastering contractor, with a heart of gold. In addition to preparing George's annual trading accounts, I would, every two months or so, write-up his formal books of account, principally a cash book, so, for a small-time plastering contractor, his accounting records were quite impressive. This was subsequently to prove to be valuable evidence. As was the common practice in the trade, George employed a number of labour-only sub-contractors. One of these sub-contractors took George to a tribunal to argue that he, the sub-contractor, was really an employee, and not self-employed. If the claimant was successful, the implications for George were serious. He would be responsible for the sub-contractors tax and national insurance liabilities, and this could go back for several years. I attended the tribunal with George, and presented the records, on his behalf, which clearly showed the weekly payments described as contractual, and which were supported by signed receipts. It carried the day, and George was later to tell me that the disgruntled sub-contractor had advised his associates 'not to cross George's barrack room lawyer'; which I hope was meant to be a compliment. After the tribunal hearing, it had been on a Saturday morning, George took me to a local pub, where we drank any number of pints of beer followed by large whisky chasers. He then, I don't know how, drove me home. Barbara had cooked pork chops for lunch. In the afternoon, I became violently ill. I blamed the pork chops. I have not eaten pork since.

It must have been Vic Child who introduced me to Bert Cresswell. Bert was a dealer in used motor cars. He had a showroom in Fallowfield, which was in South Manchester, not too far from Withington. He also had tax problems. His experience had followed a path with which I was now familiar. A new business is established; after perhaps two years, it appears on the Revenue's radar; they send out tax returns; these are ignored; after several reminders, to which they receive no response, the Revenue raise estimated assessments; these are also ignored; final demands are issued for the payment of the outstanding tax; panic sets in. Bert Cresswell was now at the panic stage. Bert had, in fact, paid the tax which had been demanded for his first year of trading based on the estimated assessment. But this only encouraged the Revenue. In the continued absence of accounts, and perhaps in the belief that they must have been too lenient for the first year, they had, not unreasonably, substantially upped the ante for the subsequent two years. The sums now being demanded – 'finally' demanded – amounted to more than £2,000 – serious money. Which is when he came to see me.

I went through the usual routine with the local Inspector of Taxes, and he agreed to accept late appeals against all three assessments, even for the first year's assessment on which the tax had already been paid. But he was insistent that the trading accounts be presented within a very short time-frame. In order to meet the tight deadline, Barbara worked with me sifting through the bank statements, invoices (many of them stained, perhaps some were blood-stains we speculated), and other detritus of a second-hand car trader. There were shoe boxes and carrier bags filled to the brim with many hundreds of pieces of paper, which we had to sort, painstakingly, into some form of order. Each item was then entered on analysis sheets, and extended into the appropriate expenses column. When the completed accounts were submitted, I was eventually able to reach an agreement with the Inland Revenue which meant that Bert had no further tax to pay. In fact, he was entitled to a small refund from the tax paid on his first year's trading.

My fee for the work I had done, with Barbara's help, was around £50; but Bert had a novel way as to how to deal with it. I did not then have a car of my own; the Ford Popular had been sold, as a necessary economy measure, at the time of the purchase of the Lynway Drive house. Bert said that he had a car which was worth more than £300, but which he could let me have for a payment in cash of £150; the difference would take care of the fee. It seemed a terrific deal. I was effectively being paid £150 for £50 of work. And the car was a second-hand Humber Hawk, not quite as flash as my father-in-law's Humber Super-Snipe, but still very smart. I gave Bert the money (from a bank loan), and took delivery of the car. For the next few weeks, I was able to drive to my Accrington constituency in my new pride and joy. It did not last long. One evening, when I was at home, the doorbell rang, and the man standing at the door told me that he had come to repossess my car. There was an outstanding hire purchase liability. He showed me all the documents, and then calmly took the keys, and drove the car away.

I cannot remember ever in my life – before or since – being so angry. I had been conned. Perhaps the deal, at the time, should have been seen as being too good to be true. But he really had seemed genuinely appreciative of the fact that I had saved him from impending catastrophe, and that he had wanted to show his gratitude. I had trusted him. I telephoned Bert who claimed to know nothing about any hire purchase debt. But he did not seem to be particularly fazed by what, for me, was a financial disaster. I guessed it was not the first time he had come across hire purchase repossessions. He said that I was not to worry, as he would either get another car for me or repay the money. He promised to speak to me again the next day. I did not hear from him. When I tried to contact him, I was told that he was not at home, and he was no longer to be found at the Fallowfield showroom. This provoked a barrage of calls from me to his wife, who was well aware of the background and the reason for my fury; but he was never there, or so she claimed. I was determined that Bert Cresswell was not going to get away with this, but was unsure as to how I could bring him to account. I was certain that recourse to the law would not be the right approach. It would be expensive and time consuming, with an uncertain outcome. I embarked upon a programme of harassment; an early form of stalking, which might have involved certain risks. I was able to borrow a car from Alys Gregory, and I drove to his home in Sale. It was a comfortable, detached house, and his wife, who I had not met before, answered the door-bell. She said that Bert was not at home, and that she did not know when he might return. She was an attractive woman, and loyal to her husband, but she must have been aware of his character defects. I said that I would wait until he returned. She did not ask me into the house, so I sat in the car, waiting, for the next two hours. No Bert. I repeated the exercise the next night. Again no Bert. I told his wife that I would return every day, until he showed his face. The following day he telephoned. He promised that, within the week, I would have a new car. It was a new Morris mini-van, and it was more than full compensation for the work I had carried out, the cash I had paid, and the grief I had suffered. But I did not act for him again.

Other clients included a shopkeeper, a publican, a driving school, and a flyweight championship boxer – 'the mighty atom'. Barbara's father, in the year before his death, also became a client, as did one of his patients. I was surprised at how modest Dr Greenbaum's income was, given that he was a senior consultant at two hospitals, and also had his private practice at 61 Palatine Road. I hope that this disclosure does not breach the rules on client confidentiality. When I left Manchester for London in May 1969, I was able to sell my mini-practice to a former colleague from J. Morris & Co. He agreed to pay me, for three years, 50 per cent of the fee income which he received from my former clients. It was a profitable climax to a venture which, for ten years, had provided a valuable source of additional income. It had paid for holidays, and other little luxuries, which we would, otherwise, have been unable to afford.

3. Carborundum

My departure from the CWS was less traumatic than my parting from J. Morris & Co. It had for some time had an air of inevitability. Towards the end of 1961, after responding to a newspaper advertisement, I joined the central accounting department of The Carborundum Co. Ltd. It was shortly before my twenty-sixth birthday, and I had been a qualified accountant for just over a year. I was to spend the next eight years commuting to Trafford Park, an enormous, sprawling industrial estate, to the west of Manchester, where Carborundum had its UK headquarters. Well known neighbours were Metropolitan-Vickers, and Kellogg's. Manchester United's football ground was nearby, as was the Lancashire County Cricket Club.

Carborundum had been founded in America by Edward Acheson in 1890. He had been seeking to develop a process, using electricity, for the manufacture of artificial diamonds, but had settled for the abrasive, diamond-like qualities of silicon carbide, the world's first man-made mineral, on which the fortunes of Carborundum were to be established. In 1895, the company moved its business to Niagara Falls, the source of energy being crucial, which is where it was still based. It was listed on the US stock exchange. Its UK subsidiary was established in Trafford Park in 1913, and there were other outposts throughout the world. It manufactured abrasives, principally forming and finishing products – grinding wheels and coated materials – and its main customers were in the automotive, steel, and aeronautical industries. It was best known to the general public through its consumer products, carborundum stones and wet and dry sandpaper, but also because of the mock Latin aphorism *illegitimi non carborundum*, the rough translation of which was 'don't let the bastards grind you down'.

The thing which first struck me at Carborundum was the number of accountants it employed. In all, there were 12 qualified accountants, which, for a manufacturing company with a workforce of around two thousand, seemed disproportionate. The managing director was an accountant, the controller (chief financial officer) was, as you would expect, an accountant, but there were also ten others. I was the newest recruit. I assumed that this was the American way of doing things, but was later to find that this was not the case; it was very much a Carborundum UK feature.

George McKenzie, the managing director, was responsible for this development, and the policy seemed to have worked, because the British company was the most profitable of the world-wide operations. McKenzie was a sleek, shy, well-barbered man, who inspired fear in all of his subordinates. He was later to be involved in a messy divorce, which featured in the *News of the World*. He seemed to have an innate distrust of non-accountants, and any issue which might be brought to his attention had to have an accountant's endorsement before he would give it any consideration. The controller, and, effectively, McKenzie's deputy, was Terry Peterson, a sallow complexioned, dapper man, who could easily have been mistaken for an Italian. He was a person of high nervous energy – he seemed to be in perpetual motion – and he had an ambitious wife. He was reputed never to contribute to a leaving present for a departing colleague. 'I would prefer to give to those who are staying,' he would say. But it did not seem that he gave much to those either. I had a desk in the general accounting department, outside Peterson's office.

My first involvement was in the product development and research areas, where I had responsibility for financial control, and helped to develop pricing policy for new products. These responsibilities were soon widened, and, gradually, I was able to gain experience of every aspect of a basic manufacturing business; often spending time with supervisors and managers on the shop floor. Each month, the financial statements were sent to Niagara Falls with an explanatory letter. It became one of my duties to draft this letter which would then be sent out under Peterson's name. The challenge was, to ensure that it would not require any change.

Sophisticated systems of financial control already existed at Carborundum, and I was not about to re-invent the wheel. But I sought to take things a stage further. Creative accounting is now a discredited term, given fresh traction by recent events at Tesco. But there are ways in which accounts can be used in an imaginative way, other than by the simple creation of illusory profits. I liked the challenge of de-mystifying accounting, making it more understandable to my non-accounting colleagues, and demonstrating how it could be used as an aid in making business decisions; in a creative manner.

Carborundum's main competitors in Britain were Norton Abrasives, also a subsidiary of an American parent, and Universal Abrasives, which was a listed UK company.

An unofficial cartel existed between these manufacturers (a little like the book trade and the Net Book Agreement, with which I was later to become so familiar), and secret meetings would take place to determine the elements of the official price lists. However, this time unlike the old book trade, individual deals were struck with large customers, particularly with the motor car manufacturers. Here, accurate costing, including, for example, the use of marginal costing techniques, was crucial. To take a simple example, the unit costs of a production run of, say, 100 are obviously higher than the unit costs of 1,000. None of this was earth shattering, but then few things are. The important thing was to get it right; particularly when quoting for large volumes.

The development of methods for performance-related pay at Carborundum, became one of my particular specialities. This was not an idea which I introduced, as the philosophy of paying people by results had already been warmly embraced. But, again, I was to take the concept much further, and into every part of the business. At its simplest and purist, performance-related pay is seen on the shop floor in the form of piece-work, where an operative does not receive an hourly rate, but is paid according to the number of units of production (widgets) which he turns out, and which involves the use of work measurement techniques. I was to extend this principle into managerial, administrative, and service areas. Every department had its own performance objectives expressed in financial terms; the trick was to break this down to the smallest possible unit, so that each employee felt that he or she could personally influence performance. Each individual was a participant in a tailor-made bonus scheme. For senior management, the key measure of performance was return on investment; profits expressed as a percentage of the total capital employed (equity plus debt) in the business. I believed this to be a much better indicator of financial health than the more familiar earnings per share calculation, which can be manipulated by levels of gearing (debt), but which is still the favourite tool of many stock market followers. What a hornet's nest bonuses have now turned out to be, with prominent City figures scratching each other's backs through the production of convoluted schemes designed to deliver rewards which bear little relationship to underlying performance; enriching themselves, impoverishing their shareholders, and discrediting the whole process.

The Niagara Falls bosses liked to keep up with what they thought to be the cutting edge of academic developments in management practice and theory. Occasionally, a Harvard professor would be shipped over to host a seminar on 'management by objectives,' or whatever else was the latest fad. I took the opportunity of one of these visits to prepare a paper of my own. It was christened, 'return on total resources.' I argued that the traditional measure of return on investment included only one of the elements which are required in an enterprise, capital, and ignored the other, labour. I devised a new formula which included the cost of labour. Profits were now to be expressed as a percentage of the sum total of capital employed and the cost of labour; the return on total resources. I prepared a table showing these new ratios for other leading UK companies, and published a small explanatory booklet. Carborundum came top of the table, so I suppose that it was all a little self-serving. It does not seem to have made any lasting impact on academia.

In 1965, George McKenzie became chairman of The Carborundum Co. Ltd., and Terry Peterson was promoted to joint managing director; Bill Whatmore, a ceramicist, shared this role with him. Whatmore was the only non-accountant in the higher echelons, but it was still clear to me, if not necessarily to him, that the accountants ruled the roost. I succeeded Peterson as controller, and was now the next in line, in the order of command. I had leapfrogged longer-serving and older colleagues, and it would not have been surprising if some might have felt that I was a little young for the job. I was still short of my thirtieth birthday. Carborundum had a works canteen, a staff dining room, a managers' dining room, and an executive dining room. I was now entitled to lunch in the executive dining room, which had its own chef to cater for the, usually, no more than four or five diners. It was five-star elitism; far from the egalitarianism which might have been expected from an American owned company.

My new role, in addition to the increased responsibility, involved a certain amount of social activity. Carborundum was very convivial. There were five divisions, shortly to become six, and each had its own social club, and special events, with Christmas, inevitably, being a particularly busy time. I was expected to attend many of these functions, often with Barbara. In addition, the controller, traditionally, hosted a dinner dance, for which I was now responsible, and which was the main event of the year. I was still very much involved politically, was having to manage my small clutch of private clients, and there was never enough time for the family. The annual summer holiday, therefore, assumed a huge importance.

Each August, following very much in the traditions of Barbara's own family, we would drive from Manchester to Lydd in Kent. Here the car would be loaded onto a rickety plane, which seemed little more than an over-sized tin box. The plane would then appear to have great difficulty in taking-off, as it wheezed and rattled across the tarmac, before completing, with some surprise, the noisy, and sometimes terrifying trip to Le Touquet. We would stay in France overnight, on our way to Italy. We would have booked accommodation at a popular holiday resort, usually Diano Marina (where Barbara had been with her parents) or Lido de Jesolo. This would be after the exchange of several letters with the hotelier, as one did at that time. But we did not reserve rooms for the overnight stops. We never had a problem; we always found a welcoming hotel-keeper, and we had with us our three boys, who, on the first trip, were only two, three and four. We stayed in modest hotels, but were always well looked after; Italians love young children. I remember, in Diano Marina, walking past a neighbouring hotel, which was only slightly superior to our own, and looking enviously, through its dining room windows, at tables laid out for dinner, with half-full bottles of wine, and with the corks re-inserted. It is a sight which would now horrify me, but, at the time, wine with dinner was a luxury which we could not yet afford.

In 1967, Carborundum acquired W. T. Copeland and Sons Ltd., the manufacturers of Spode fine china. Carborundum had long been seeking to diversify. Its markets were highly cyclical, being very reliant on capital goods, and technological change was creating a new vulnerability. Engineering precision, which traditionally could only be achieved by the use of grinding wheels, was now being brought about by improved computer technology, which had an accuracy which could remove the need for any further correction. And it was thought that china fitted into Carborundum's core ceramics technology.

Nonetheless, it seemed a very odd purchase. There was only a tenuous link between the manufacture of grinding wheels and the production of delicate tableware. Such an esoteric acquisition was more likely to have been inspired by reasons of opportunism or personal aggrandisement; Spode would make a better dinner party conversation piece than abrasives. I had not been involved in the negotiations for the acquisition, but I was now responsible for introducing Carborundum systems into this new jewel in our crown. I was also given a general oversight of its performance, though I did not have operational responsibility. It was a sort of non-executive chairman's role. My new routine now included a weekly visit to Spode's factory in Stoke-on-Trent.

In the late spring of 1968, one of the smaller Wall Street stockbroking firms organised a tour of some of the European financial centres, to introduce a number of its mid-market clients to potential investors. Carborundum was one of the clients, but its representative, rather late in the day, had withdrawn, and I was deputed to be his last minute replacement. It was to be an eye-opener. We travelled first class, stayed at the Plaza Athénée in Paris, the Hotel Amigo in Brussels, and the Savoy in London. For the others there was little new in this. They were independently wealthy, entrepreneurial chief executives of companies which they or their families had founded, and of which they were still part owners. Nonetheless, they were more than happy to exploit the very generous hospitality of their hosts. They all drank too much, and were much more interested in having a good time, rather than in saving themselves to impress investors. At each stop there were presentations to the local financial community, and my own, inevitably, was confined to the activities of Carborundum's UK subsidiary, which was the extent of my knowledge and experience; but it was not difficult to shine in such dissolute company, and the inclusion of Spode might have given my contribution a glamorous edge. When it was all over, and I had said goodbye to my new, and now even more heavily hung-over friends, the stockbroking partner said that he would be speaking to Bill Wendell, Carborundum's president. He made it clear that he would be giving a favourable report. Two weeks later I received a summons to visit Wendell in Niagara Falls.

I had already been to America several times on Carborundum business and had long ago exhausted my small supply of tired jokes about differences between the two countries; the problems of a supposedly common language, the fact that politicians in America run for office whilst in Britain they stand. I had met Bill Wendell at receptions (he also seemed to drink a lot, perhaps it was an American thing) but had never had a proper conversation with him. Now, I had a face-to-face meeting, alone, in his office. He was relaxed, warm and friendly. He said that they had a job for me here in Niagara Falls. I would report to a senior vice president, who in turn reported to Wendell. I was to talk to all the key people at headquarters, and take as long as I wanted in making my decision. Whatever my answer, he said, nothing would be held against me. The job on offer was to be the controller of Carborundum's largest division, and it would be based in Niagara Falls. It was bigger in scale than the Manchester job, but the basic ingredients were the same. It would not greatly add to my experience, apart from the fact that I would be working in a new country; and I was not sure that I would enjoy the same autonomy. Niagara is on the Canadian border, in upstate New York, and the nearest large town is Buffalo; it had little to offer apart from

130

the background mood-music of the waterfalls. It was small-town America, and I had already tasted the delights, if only fleetingly, of Paris, New York and London. I turned the job down.

But the experience had unsettled me. And I had now come to the attention of the head-hunters. My ideas on payment by results, and on a more practical approach to the use of accounting techniques, meant that I had been asked to speak at a number of seminars at the University of Manchester and at Management Centre Europe, in Brussels; and I had recently been the subject of a feature page article in the *Financial Times* on our use of incentive schemes. Which is when the head-hunters called. There were two people in London they wished me to meet. One of them was very persuasive. A new future beckoned.

4. Pentos

I had very mixed feelings about leaving Carborundum. I had many friends there, and was respected. And I had spent my entire life living and working in Manchester. A change of job always involves risk, but a move to a new job in a new city, London, whilst potentially exciting, compounded the risks of the unknown. An arm around the shoulder, and a promise of riches to come, from the Carborundum hierarchy, might easily have prompted second thoughts. But it didn't happen. Copeland's gave me a very handsome, specially inscribed, blue and gold decorated Spode bowl, and there were other parting gifts, although I doubt that Terry Peterson broke his lifetime ban on contributions for leavers. Our house was put on the market – we now lived in the more up-market area of Hale, in Cheshire, and after its sale, and the repayment of the mortgage, we were left with £3,000. A net worth of £3,000 was not much reward for ten years of hard labour, but it was a definite improvement on zero.

We purchased a house in Hampstead Garden Suburb, it was April 1969, and, as our own money was needed for furnishings and improvements, we again had to borrow the deposit, but this time from my new employer. The new house cost £22,500, exactly ten times the cost of our first home ten years ago. My starting salary in the new job was £7,500 (a 50 per cent improvement on my final salary at Carborundum), which was again a multiple of ten over my salary at the time of the first house purchase. An elegant symmetry.

The person who had persuaded me to leave Manchester for London was Pat Matthews, the charismatic but volatile head of First National Finance Corporation (FNFC). He had built a successful financial services group over a short period of time, from a motor car hire purchase base. It had expanded rapidly into property (both as a principal and as a lender), and into stock market investment. It had also acquired an issuing house which could help new companies to obtain a stock market quotation. It was one of the swashbuckling enterprises, in the heady, go-go days of the late 60s and early 70s, described dismissively by the City establishment as 'secondary banks'. The job which Pat offered me was in two parts; to establish new systems of financial control, and to be responsible for a new subsidiary, which would include the issuing house, and which would make strategic investments in other quoted companies where, hopefully, my involvement would help to improve performance. It was the second part of the job which had caught my imagination.

It was an entirely new world. I had never had any dealings with the City before, and knew nothing of its ways or of its people. But, with the help of good fortune, I was soon to make my mark. I acquired shareholdings in two quoted companies, on behalf of FNFC, and was able to exercise some influence; their fortunes improved. I joined FNFC's main board, as corporate finance director, and established good working relationships with some of the influential people in the City, stockbrokers, fund managers, corporate lawyers, and investigating accountants. Pat had introduced me to the City, and had given me a marvellous opportunity, but he was not the easiest of colleagues. A deteriorating personal relationship, and some siren voices from my new friends, led to the formation of my own investment company. After two and a half years with FNFC, I was soon to be on my own.

I have written about Pentos at some length in my business memoir, *Against My Better Judgement*, which was published in 1994. But, for the sake of completeness, and, after such a long period of time, perhaps being able to offer a more detached and mature reflection, I will again seek to paint the scene, but this time using a broader brush. I can hardly write a personal memoir without mentioning something which was to dominate more than 21 years of my life.

Pentos was formed as a typical 'off the-shelf' company with £100 capital. It was thought that the name could be changed to something more appropriate at a later date, but we took to the name, and it stuck. With my secretary, and another colleague from FNFC, I took an office at 1 New Bond Street, which was to become the Pentos headquarters, and where I was to stay for almost 20 years. The building is now occupied by the American fashion house, Ralph Lauren.

In May 1972, I was able to arrange a reverse take-over of an existing public company, The Cape Town and District Gas Light and Coke Company Limited, and its name was then changed to Pentos. Within four months of its formation, Pentos had a stock market listing in its own right, and I, at the age of 37, was its chairman and chief executive.

The colleague who came with me from FNFC was William Sanders, who was to become very helpful in developing important relationships with the City. William was an old Etonian, and former Guards officer. His background could not have been more different from my own. An education at Eton College had long been seen as a passport to a charmed life. But there was a time, in the 70s and 80s, when it became to be seen as almost an impediment. It was thought that, with 'big bang,' and a more egalitarian and anti-toff world, the privileged 'old-boy' network had gone forever. The pendulum has now swung back with a vengeance. Old Etonians are again top-dogs. In Britain, the government and the establishment are again dominated by those who went to the best and most expensive schools. The loss of our grammar schools is felt even more keenly. A neighbour in the country has her son at Eton. I said to her recently, 'I hope that he has some normal friends, from ordinary backgrounds, and that they are not all from Eton.' 'Oh yes,' she replied, 'he has some friends who are at Harrow.' You couldn't make it up. Some of my own current friends went to Eton, and, as my Auntie Betty might have put it, they are not all bad people.

The Pentos story can be told as a game of two halves, and as a tale of three recessions. Pentos looked to invest in markets which were fragmented, with no dominant player. We were concerned with quality, a recognisable product, the potential for market leadership, and a clear brand identity. The twin corporate objectives, which were first published in the initial annual report, and which were repeated in every succeeding year, were 'to earn a return on investment which is significantly better than average, and to seek leadership and a clear identity in its chosen markets.' Marketing flair was as important as financial expertise.

The first half of the story covers the period from the formation of Pentos to the end of the decade. The businesses in which we first invested usually had some kind of engineering involvement, which was relevant to my own experience at Carborundum, although we also made a start in the book trade, which was later to become so important. A good example of our approach can be seen with Halls garden buildings, which we had acquired with the purchase of the Austin Hall Group. Halls was a well-known name in a fragmented market, but little had been done to exploit brand awareness. Sales were achieved mainly by mail order. In 1974 we decided to manufacture an aluminium greenhouse to sell alongside the traditional cedar product. The aluminium greenhouse was cheaper, and could be packaged and sold in the high street like any other consumer product. Within a year, aluminium greenhouse sales had overtaken cedar, the total number of greenhouse sales doubled, and Halls had the dominant position, with more than 40 per cent market share. In 1977, Halls won the Institute of Marketing award for outstanding achievement in British marketing.

In the tables published to celebrate the end of the decade of the '70s, Pentos was ranked the third best performing company in the stock market as a whole, and third in earnings per share growth. £10,000 invested in Pentos in 1972 was now, with dividend income reinvested, worth

£250,000. But storm clouds were gathering. The second half of the Pentos story was to prove much more turbulent.

During Pentos's first experience of recession in1973-75, it emerged relatively unscathed. The oil price explosion had precipitated a major meltdown in world financial markets; the *Financial Times* ordinary share index, which had peaked at more than 500, touched a low of 146 in January 1975. The main victims of this turmoil were in the financial sector – my former employer, FNFC, was one of them – and in commercial property, where values fell by up to one half. The National Westminster Bank had to issue a press statement to say that it was financially sound.

The recession of 1980-82 was of a different sort; it was of unparalleled severity in terms of its relative concentration on one sector, and in one part of the country. It hit people who worked in factories and who lived in the North. The industrial heartlands became industrial wastelands. Most of Pentos's businesses were in the Midlands and the North. We were badly hit, and, to add to our discomfort, our borrowings were too high. We embarked on a programme of disposing of peripheral assets and businesses, whilst seeking to protect our perceived 'crown jewels' from the risk of a fire sale. We were to shed our conglomerate identity, and develop a slimmed-down business into a more focused specialist retailer.

Things did not always go smoothly. On 27 March 1980, I was having lunch on an outside restaurant terrace in St. Moritz after a morning's skiing, when an American, hearing my English voice, leaned over my table to speak to me. 'Have you heard the news about Bunker Hunt,' he asked. I hadn't. He told me that Hunt, who with his brother, Herbert, had been seeking to corner the international silver market, was effectively broke. Apparently, regulators had moved in, and the price of silver had plummeted. The Hunts were reputed to have lost more than one billion dollars. He would have had no idea how devastating that news was for me. Pentos owned Barker Ellis, a manufacturing silversmiths, based in Birmingham. Before leaving London I had agreed its sale to a trade buyer, and it was an important part of our asset disposal programme. A key condition of the sale related to the price of silver. I quickly returned to my hotel to telephone the office. I was able to confirm my informant's story, and it soon became clear that the deal was off. Sometime later the business was sold to its management, but at a much, much reduced price.

There were a number of other hiccups along the way, but, by the end of 1984, the borrowings had been almost eliminated, and we were able to launch a rights issue to help finance the expansion of our retailing brands, Dillons, Athena and Ryman into prominent positions on Britain's high streets.

I have for most of my life been keen on sport, although I have never been particularly good at it. My early health problems meant that my participation started later than for most people, so that it was always unlikely that I could ever have become more than proficient. Now, in my eightieth year, people see me still playing tennis and skiing, and assume that I must, at one time, have been quite good. They are wrong. But I am competitive, and I do enjoy it. Soon after my arrival in London, several of my new City friends persuaded me to join them in what had become a regular Sunday game of football in Hyde Park. It was little more than a kick-around, with coats for goal-posts, and pick-up teams selected from the disparate group of people who found themselves at a loose-end on a Sunday morning. But it was all taken deadly seriously. After the game we would all enjoy a pint of beer in a local pub, and re-live the highlights. Two of our sons, Anthony and Jeremy would sometimes join me, but Nicholas preferred fishing. Victor Blank, a friend, who acted for Pentos as a corporate lawyer and was later to become a non-executive director, was also an occasional player. He was a 'goal-hanger', who positioned himself as close as possible to the goalkeeper, in the hope of scrambling the ball home. We did not apply the offside rules. As I approached my fiftieth birthday, my lack of pace and skill meant that I was repeatedly getting my shins kicked by faster, 21-year-old Italian waiters, who were much better players. I took up tennis, which became the newest of what were to be my twin (until bridge came on the scene to make it three) continuing passions. The other twin passion was skiing. I was taught to ski when the Swiss over-complicated things. It was one position for the shoulder, one for the hips, skis close together, and a lot of falling down. Now it is simpler. Relax, bend your knees, and change your weight from ski to ski; much easier; but perhaps not so profitable for the ski-school. We first went to Switzerland for winter sports in 1970, and, however intense the business pressures were at one time, we have not missed a year since.

Dillons was easily the most significant of the three retailing chains within Pentos, although Athena and Ryman were also important and profitable businesses, meeting our operating criteria of having a clear brand identity and market leadership. Dillons on many occasions became the story; which was not always helpful. Having a high profile can create its own problems. But it was a very special story.

Over a period of ten years, the business expanded from a single university bookshop to a national chain of 100 bookshops, with 550,000 square feet of retail space, and annual sales of more than £150 million. It was Britain's largest specialist bookseller, accounted for twelve per cent of the UK book market, and, according to independent research, was the country's best known and highest regarded book chain. We had established a strong, strategic presence within book retailing, which we believed would produce long term benefits for Pentos shareholders.

Our activities did not always meet with the approval of the book trade establishment. The prominent position which I took in opposition to the Net Book Agreement did not help. As a liberal, I would be expected to be against restrictive practices, but the price control of books also conflicted with our own commercial interests. It prevented us from using normal marketing tools to promote book sales, get more customers into bookshops, and, of course, offer lower prices to the book buyer. The Publishers Association fought us tooth and nail, and at one stage sought to have me imprisoned for contempt of court; they finished up paying our legal costs. The trade magazine, *The Bookseller*, was consistently hostile and at times venomous, although, after the acquisition of Hatchard's, and when I became the official bookseller to the Queen, it was moved to write, 'Even those booksellers who detest Mr Maher's stance on the Net Book Agreement will concur – however grudgingly – that the new bookseller to the royal family has done more for the quality of bookshops in this country than anyone else in the last decade and he will almost certainly turn Hatchard's into a shop fit to hold the royal warrants which it had ceased to be under its previous owner.'

My role in the campaign to abolish price control on books had brought me to the attention of the Institute of Economic Affairs. It is an influential and highly regarded think-tank, and I was now one of its mini heroes. In 1989, it organised a lunch, to which I was invited, to celebrate the 25th anniversary of the Resale Prices Act, which had abolished resale price maintenance. Ted Heath, when he was President of the Board of Trade in Harold Macmillan's government, had been its sponsor. He was now the principal guest at lunch. When he arrived, he immediately rushed over to me to ask, in a gauche manner, 'Are you the new big man here?' He had mistaken me for Graham Mather, who had recently taken over as Director General of the IEA from its *éminence grise*, Ralph Harris. I pointed him in the right direction. For a former prime minister, Heath was remarkably awkward and ill at ease. He made a short speech after lunch in which he emphasised his bravery in pushing through the legislation despite the Macmillan's family strong interest in publishing. He seemed to have forgotten that books had been exempted from the Resale Prices Act, and that this was what I had been seeking to put right, and was the reason for my presence.

In my business dealings, over many years, I found that most people, in every walk of life, and at every level, were usually well-intentioned. We did not always agree, in fact there were sometimes sharply expressed disagreements, and we did not always become friends; but it was rare to make enemies. There were a couple of notable exceptions. One was Robert Maxwell. He did not have a single redeeming feature. I told the story of Maxwell and his writs in 1989, in *Against my Better Judgement*, but it was to have an interesting coda, and its essentials merit re-telling. Tom Bower had written an unflattering biography, *Maxwell the Outsider*, and Maxwell was incensed. In his usual bullying style, he issued writs for defamation, and then followed them up with aggressive letters to booksellers, including Dillons, threatening the most dire consequences if we dared to sell the book. Dillons had always resisted any attempts to impose censorship, and the book remained on sale. It later emerged that we were alone amongst booksellers in taking this stand. Shortly afterwards, we experienced difficulty in obtaining supplies of books from publishing companies owned by Maxwell, primarily Macdonald's. One Sunday morning, I received a telephone call from Robert Peston, then a journalist on the *Independent*. He told me that he understood that we were 'on stop' with Macdonald's, on instructions from Maxwell, because of our failure to pay the account, and asked for my comments. I told Peston, correctly, that 'we do not owe him a cent.' We discussed other possible reasons for the supply problems, and the Bower biography was mentioned. Peston allowed this speculation to spill over into his article the following day. The full fury of Maxwell was to follow. I received a ferocious letter signed by one of the Maxwell sons, but in the poisonous style of the father. I spoke to Peter Jay, the former British ambassador to Washington, and the son-in-law of a former British prime minister, who was then Maxwell's aide-de-camp, in the hope of bringing some sanity into the situation. Jay was icily cold, unfriendly, detached. The inevitable writs followed; one for me, one for Peston, and one for Andreas Whittam Smith, the editor of the *Independent*. The writs were for defamation, although my lawyers advised me that I was the person who had been defamed. But that was how Maxwell behaved. Victor Blank, now on the Pentos board, offered to mediate, as he

141

knew Maxwell slightly. He returned from his meeting on noticeably more friendly terms with 'Captain Bob', as he called him, but it was not obvious that he had progressed our cause. Negotiations with Maxwell were always time consuming and often counter-productive. On this occasion, before the dispute was finally resolved, he met his death when he disappeared from his yacht. Few tears were shed.

The coda to the Maxwell story involved Peter Jay. Some two years after the events I have set out above, I was invited to one of Jeffrey Archer's 'over the top' lunch parties. I was placed next to Jay. He checked my name, and asked with a quizzical look, 'Do we know each other?' I reminded him of our telephone conversation. He did not seem best pleased. Some further years later, I was again placed next to him, this time at dinner, at a club, where I was a new member. We went through the same routine. He asked the same question, and I gave the same answer. He looked uncomfortable, sighed heavily, and we moved on. It did not seem to be a pleasant memory; and he had clearly been terrified of Maxwell.

There is a further vignette involving Maxwell. I was invited to a charity lunch, hosted by Lord Boardman, the chairman of the National Westminster Bank. The venue was the recently opened NatWest Tower. As I entered the lift to go to the top floor, I saw that there were three other occupants on the same mission: Robert Maxwell; Alan Bond, the Australian businessman and America's Cup winner, who was later to spend some years in prison for fraud; and Gerald Ronson, the property developer, who was also to spend some time in prison as a result of his unfortunate involvement in the 'Guinness Affair', and in which many people thought that he was the fall-guy in an establishment stitch-up. Each was slumped, arms akimbo, in a different corner of the lift. I stepped tentatively into the centre and, as we sped swiftly to the top of the Tower to the pre-lunch reception, not a single word was spoken.

The recession of 1991 to 1993 was the longest and deepest of them all. It was made worse by Britain's membership of the Exchange Rate Mechanism. Interest rates were at record levels, and retail sales took the hit, as heavily indebted consumers battened down the hatches, and householders sought to cope with the new phenomenon of 'negative equity.' And Pentos's borrowings were again too high. We had continued to invest throughout the recession as opportunities arose, particularly for new Dillons bookshops, which we thought we might not see again. With the benefit of hindsight, the pace of new investment was probably a mistake; an error of judgement on my part. But we were taking a long term view which required time and patience. The recession would eventually end, and the abolition of the Net Book Agreement would give us fresh marketing opportunities to exploit from our dominant position. Unfortunately, the City had become even more obsessed with the short term than was usual. Patience was in short supply. There were increasing questions about policy; and about what was perceived to be my authoritarian management style. There was always some, often anonymous, figure in the book trade who would make some disobliging comment to the press and help to feed the rumour mill of the City. As Machiavelli wrote in *The Prince*, 'the reformer has enemies in all those who profit by the old order and only lukewarm defenders in all those who would profit by the new.'

I was, nonetheless, surprised and shocked when, in September 1993, the non-executive directors, led by Victor Blank, who was later to become chairman of Trinity Mirror, the publisher of the *Daily Mirror*, and then chairman of Lloyds Bank, asked me to step down. Although Victor pulled the trigger, it is not totally clear, even at this distance, who supplied the bullet. When the news broke, Schroder's, our merchant bank, called to say that it was the last thing that Win Bischoff, its chief executive had wanted. The Midland Bank conveyed the same message; as did our stockbrokers. The most likely candidate was Carol Galley of Mercury Asset Management (MAM). MAM was our largest institutional shareholder. They had been enthusiastic supporters since our earliest days, first under the leadership of Leonard Licht, then under Nicola Horlick. I was unaware of Carol Galley, until meeting her at a lunch at 11 Downing Street. She introduced herself to me as Pentos's major shareholder. I appeared mystified, and she was clearly miffed that I did not know who she was. She thought I did not know who our shareholders were; even the most important one. She had recently been flexing her muscles in targeting entrepreneurial business leaders who she considered had got a little above themselves. Perhaps she thought I fell into that category. Sometime later she expressed her misgivings to Schroder's, and they suggested to me that I should meet her. However, when I went to MAM's offices for a routine briefing, she did not put in an appearance. I have not seen her again since that one fleeting moment, before lunch, in Downing Street. Victor Blank would certainly have been prepared to do her bidding. He was anxious to burnish his credentials as the 'tough guy' in the boardroom, and in a newspaper interview, some months later, he was to boast that his 'friendship' with the chairman of Pentos had not prevented him doing his duty. It was Victor who delivered the message, either from conviction, or as a proxy.

Sir Kit McMahon, who had been the deputy chairman of the Bank of England and the former chairman of the Midland Bank, was the other independent non-executive director of Pentos, and he succeeded me as chairman. Within two years of my departure, despite raising £45 million of new money from shareholders, Pentos was broken up, and the company, which I founded and then managed for more than 20 years, was no more.

I did not get rich from Pentos. I was well paid, but I did not realise the rewards from my shareholding which at one time seemed likely. When I left, the Pentos share price was significantly below its peak, but it was still more than ten times higher than at its starting point; and there had been dividends along the way.

The scale of my remuneration did not remotely match the obscene levels of pay which are now seen as normal for the heads of quite modest public companies; even partners in City law firms, hardly wealth creators, now take home, I hesitate to write 'earn', more than £1 million each year. But I have no complaints; I was treated fairly. It was not that top executive pay was wrong then, it just happens to be wrong now. As Sebastian Faulks asks in *A Week in September*, 'When did the civilised man stop viewing money as a means to various enjoyable ends and start to view it as an end in itself? When did respectable people give themselves over full-time to counting zeroes?' I suppose it is legitimate to ask another question, 'Why is the market not providing a correction?' One would expect that equally qualified people would be standing in line claiming that they would do the job for half as much.

My obsession with Pentos meant that I was not as much around the house, and not as diligent in monitoring and supporting our children's education and general welfare, as I now wish had been the case. Which does not mean that Barbara, often alone, did not do a brilliant job, because she did. The three boys had become day-boys at Highgate School. We had been enthused by its inspirational headmaster at the interview stage, but, by the time the boys started at school, he had retired and been replaced by a less inspiring figure. Perhaps partly because of this, and perhaps also because of my own lack of sufficient attention to their needs, they did not do as well as they might have hoped. This is an assessment with which, I believe, they would most likely agree, but they have since more than made up for any slight disappointment by hard work and gritty determination. There have been ups and downs, but all three have been successful in pursuing their respective careers.

Shortly after the start of Pentos we had moved into a large family house in Hampstead Way (it is now occupied by the television personality, Jonathan Ross) which was not too far away from Highgate School. It had an acre of gardens, which, for a house so close to the centre of London, was unusual. In addition to running this large home (with the help of a wonderfully warm, generous-hearted, and hard-working housekeeper; at dinner parties, she would insist on serving me first in her native Poland's tradition), and establishing a beautiful garden with a wide array of exotic magnolia trees and water features, Barbara developed a new interest. It happened by chance. A neighbour with whom Barbara became close friends was Claudia Roden, a successful cookery writer. Barbara's mother had been an excellent cook in a kitchen with a strong European flavour, and Barbara had followed in her footsteps. She suggested to Claudia that there was a need for a serious book on cakes which would cover the history of the ingredients, the cooking utensils, and the traditions, as well as the end products; much, much more than a recipe book. Claudia was already fully committed but she suggested that this could be a project for Barbara. It was a surprising, but imaginative proposal, and it was spot on. And that is how Barbara became a cookery writer. She was introduced to Jill Norman, Claudia's editor at Penguin, and then spent three years – much of it at the London Library – researching and writing the book. *Cakes* was published in hardback by the imprint Jill Norman and Hobday in 1982 and in paperback by Penguin in 1984. Barbara was the joint winner, with Jane Grigson, of the André Simon Memorial Fund Book Award for 1982. It was a scholarly book which became a classic and which established Barbara's reputation. She was later to write further cookery books with Dorland Kindersley which were aimed at a wider, international, mass market.

A final Pentos postscript. When I took my last journey home, it was in November 1993, from New Bond Street to the house in the country in which we now lived, Joe, my chauffeur of many years standing, turned his head, and said to me, 'It's that Victor Blank, innit? I still 'ave connections in the East End, just give me the word, and I can 'ave 'im taken care of.' I am sure that he was only joking.

5. After Pentos

My business memoir, *Against My Better Judgement*, was published in the autumn of 1994. It was widely, and generally favourably, reviewed, was fleetingly in one of the best-sellers lists and was the subject of a BBC2 TV documentary. William Rees-Mogg wrote a generous 1,500 word op-ed column in *The Times*. He was its former editor, and I had once crossed swords with him whilst he was chairman of the Arts Council.

I have no doubt that writing the book was cathartic, but I had also really enjoyed the actual process of writing; it had whetted my appetite.

Apart from my financial and advisory roles in the business activities of two of our sons, Nicholas and Anthony, I was to have only one final entrepreneurial flourish. Towards the end of 1994, I became a major shareholder and chairman of a book publishing company, Chalford Publishing (it was later to change its name to Tempus Publishing). Chalford had a very attractive business model. It published local photographic history books. They were to a standard format, and the sepia photographs and accompanying text created a nostalgic appeal. They were, in the jargon of the book trade, 'local interest books.' The plan was to publish a book for each town within the UK. It was later to be rolled out also in Germany, France, and America. The text was provided by a local historian or librarian at very little cost as they were usually only too pleased to see their name in print. It was a form of vanity which had previously been exploited by Robert Maxwell in his early academic publishing days. The editorial costs of the books were, therefore, low. But equally attractive were the minimal distribution costs. One of the nightmares of traditional trade publishing is the fact that bookshops order such small quantities. A publisher with a print run of, say, 3,000 copies of a title would find that he was typically sending two or three copies of the book to bookshops throughout the country, and as far apart as Land's End and John O'Groats. The beauty of the Chalford formula was that the potential market was highly concentrated in the target towns, and the retail outlets would be just the local bookshop and WH Smith. The low production costs meant that the Chalford publications were viable at a print run of as little as 1,000 copies, and the orders from the customer bookshops were usually in the hundreds rather than the small units of trade publishing. Clearly there was nothing new in the concept of local interest publishing, but what was new was the professional and comprehensive approach to the market with all the books being published from the same template. It seemed, at least from my review of the business plan, to be, as the commercial television companies had once been described, 'a licence to print money.'

The founder of Chalford was Alan Sutton, a publisher with a colourful reputation, and to whom I had been introduced by an intermediary, who was acting on Sutton's behalf to raise money for his new venture. The business formula had been devised in one of his previous incarnations, and under a different imprint, Alan Sutton Publishing. The essential elements of the model had, therefore, already been tested. His original, embryonic company had run out of money and had been sold, with Sutton still in charge, to the Guernsey Press, a newspaper publisher. Sutton had soon fallen out with the new owners (I was later to find that he made a habit of quarrelling with his partners) and he had now started out again. My own investment was relatively modest. One of the other outside shareholders was the Bath Press, which was to be the printer for the books, but Sutton retained a little more than 50 per cent of the equity. I was the second largest shareholder and I had important covenants in my shareholders agreement to ensure that I had effective control on all major decisions. Those covenants were to prove extremely valuable.

After the board meeting to approve my investment and to deal with the formalities, we all had lunch together, and I then went with Sutton to his office for an informal chat. He suddenly became agitated, and passed on to me a letter which had appeared on his desk. It was from solicitors, acting for the Guernsey Press, and it claimed that Sutton's new business was guilty of 'passing off' (publishing books to which Guernsey had the rights) – and threatening a writ unless Chalford ceased publishing the offending titles with immediate effect. I felt very unwell; it seemed that I had been set up. But Sutton protested that he had been totally unaware of any problem, and that the letter was as much a surprise to him as it was to me. Fortunately, in carrying out my due diligence prior to making the investment, I had spoken to the chairman of the Guernsey Press to ask if he knew of any reason why I should not go ahead with my planned involvement with Alan Sutton. Whilst conceding that Sutton could be difficult, he gave him an otherwise clean bill of health; there was not the slightest hint of any impending legal action. I undertook to speak to Guernsey's lawyers on Sutton's behalf. I made them aware of my conversation with Guernsey's chairman. I told them that if they took out an injunction to prevent Chalford from publishing (which is what they had threatened) then I would hold their client responsible for my losses. They backed down, although we agreed to make a small contribution to their legal costs. But it could have been worse, very much worse. If I had not made that telephone call to Guernsey, Chalford could have been closed down almost before it had started.

Chalford performed well; and, on a visit to its American offices in New England, I was able to see, at first hand, that the prospects in the US were even better. I was beginning to believe that it had the potential to be a hugely successful business. But Sutton had developed a major distraction. He now had ambitions to diversify and to develop a history list as part of a traditional mainstream publishing arm; which would have all the risks and distributional problems of that notoriously fickle business. It was not what I had bought into. We had a highly profitable niche business, and I did not want to place it in jeopardy. Sutton now showed that he could be stubborn as well as difficult. Despite my objections, he pressed on with his plans and recruited a commissioning editor. But my blocking covenants meant that he could not take the matter any further without my approval. It was an impasse. His solution was to arrange a re-financing, which involved buying out the outside shareholders with borrowed money. The terms of his proposal meant that I would receive a sum equal to ten times my original investment, after a period of just over three years of involvement. This, clearly, had its attractions, but I still believed that, in the longer term, the returns could have been significantly higher. There seemed little point in seeking to repair a relationship which had irretrievably broken down, and I accepted his offer. And that was the end of my life in business.

An unkind reader might conclude that the author of this book would not be a suitable candidate for a quango; that judgement would be sound. Quangos hardly qualify as business, in fact they are its antithesis, but these few paragraphs, on my only brush with a quango, do not fit in easily, other than at the fag-end of this business chapter.

In the summer of 1996, I received an unexpected telephone call from Iain Sproat. Iain was then the Secretary of State responsible for the Department of National Heritage (later to become the Department of Culture, Media and Sport) in John Major's Conservative government. He was mad on cricket, was the editor of the annual *Cricketers' Who's Who*, and was an avid book collector, with an obsession with Pushkin. I had got to know him a little, and I liked him. The purpose of his telephone call was to discuss the opportunities for the public libraries (they were part of his responsibilities) in the light of the demise of the Net Book Agreement. I must have expressed a view on the matter on some occasion, and this had prompted Iain's call. He asked if I would be prepared to write a paper for him on the subject. I was not sure that I would be able to present my arguments in the best civil service style or format, and Iain suggested that I spoke to Alan Judd, then a civil servant but now a successful novelist, if I needed any guidance. Alan was very reassuring, and said that he was certain that anything which I prepared would make a refreshing change from the turgid prose which was the Minister's normal diet.

The paper which I submitted to Iain was headlined 'Public Libraries – a £20 million opportunity'. I explained that public libraries had long had a raw deal from the book trade, typically receiving discounts on the cover price which were 20 per cent lower than those offered to the smallest bookshop in the land. The collapse of the Net Book Agreement now gave librarians, for the first time, the freedom to negotiate terms of trade without constraint. Publishers, however, (Adam Smith would not have been surprised) were now colluding together to fight a rear-guard action and displaying their usual ferocity in defending their privileges, and in seeking to prevent the public libraries from enjoying the full benefits of open competition. Librarians, I concluded, would need to become much more aggressive in their response. The prize was a potential £20 million saving on the book purchase fund (which was in itself only ten per cent of the total spending by public libraries), and which could be used to buy more books. When Iain received the paper, he telephoned to ask, in his usual persuasive manner, if I would be prepared to become a member of the Advisory Council on Libraries; one of the dreaded quangos.

Successive governments have promised to have a 'bonfire of the quangos', but at the end of their term they have invariably created more than they have abolished. It has long been my view that this proliferation is one of the banes of public life. Populated by the same self-serving, if sometimes well-meaning, people, ostensibly trying to help, but more often making things worse. And just generally getting in the way; costing money which we cannot afford. It is enormously satisfying to have one's prejudices confirmed rather than challenged. The Advisory Council on Libraries was not to disappoint. The preamble consisted of box-ticking forms containing the usual questions with the emphasis on ethnicity and political affiliations; everything, apart from anything which might have been remotely related to my suitability for membership of a committee responsible for the nation's public libraries. Once I was on board, I was to find that my new colleagues were not the slightest bit interested in doing anything so boring as getting their hands dirty in grubby negotiations on discounts; and which might, in any event, disturb their cosy relationships with their friends in the book trade. I stayed for a little over a year; which was far too long. No more quangos.

IX
WHAT SHOULD A LIBERAL DO?

My current routine, as I walk from the Savile Club to the Portland Club, takes me, most days, past a plaque by 28 King Street, in St. James's. It commemorates the founding of the Liberal Party, at that address, on 6 June 1859. Today, we no longer have a Liberal Party. The party, for which we all fought with such youthful energy and enthusiasm for so many years, no longer exists. Its merger with the SDP – in itself a breakaway from the Labour Party – in 1988, created a new party, the Liberal Democrats.

The Liberal Party was the party of Gladstone, Asquith and Lloyd George. Of course, that was long before my time, and it was the inspirational, if sometimes unworldly, Jo Grimond who was leader when I first became an activist. Of his successors, there have been seven if we include the Liberal Democrats, only Paddy Ashdown has come close to matching Grimond's muscular, radical liberalism. Jeremy Thorpe, Grimond's immediate successor in 1967, was flash and flamboyant; the Nigel Farage of his day. Grimond must have known that Thorpe was fatally flawed, but a successor was being chosen from a not particularly wide field. When Thorpe imploded, in 1976, David Steel came along to steady the boat. Steel was a little bit like a church mouse, and he never fully recovered from his *Spitting Image* caricature as the midget in the breast pocket of his SDP counterpart David Owen's jacket. Paddy Ashdown, tough, no nonsense and down to earth, although a little star-struck by Tony Blair, became the first leader of the merged party in 1988. Then came the totally unsuitable Charles Kennedy, followed by the charming but old-before-his-time Menzies Campbell, who never had a chance. His successor, Nick Clegg, a milk and water liberal, a petulant obstructer of boundary revision and House of Lords reform, and an unthinking supporter of an unreformed European Union, has now brought the party close to extinction. And the arrival of Tim Fallon, a populist in the tradition of Charles Kennedy, but, who, in comparison, would make Kennedy appear to have been a political giant, brings that day nearer

It was a little before the merger, in 1987, that I again became actively involved in Liberal Party politics. It was after an initiative by Tim Razzall, who was the party treasurer. Since the general election campaign in Runcorn, I had continued to vote Liberal, but was no longer a party member. I had been to lunch on two occasions at the House of Commons as a guest of David Steel, but had assumed that this was because I had been targeted as a potentially friendly businessman. There was no follow up.

Tim Razzall thought that the party had been neglectful in not courting more aggressively its obvious supporters in the business community. We lunched together, and he invited me to get-to-know-you receptions where there would be other leading Liberals. After the merger, I was invited to become a trustee; there were three other trustees, including Peter Parker (a social democrat, as were most of the other important members of the newly merged party), the former chairman of British Rail, who became our chairman. Tim Razzall and Tim Clement-Jones, another senior party figure, were to attend meetings, ex-officio. Peter Parker soon christened them, 'the two Tims'. They are both now members of the House of Lords.

When I first asked about the role of the trustees, I was told that their main purpose was 'to prevent a Jeremy Thor-

155

pe situation arising again'. This was not a reference to his criminal trial for conspiracy to murder, but to funds donated by 'Union Jack' Haywood, a wealthy benefactor, which were intended for the Liberal Party, but which finished up in Mr Thorpe's bank account. At the regular trustees meeting, we would review the accounts, which were, at best, rudimentary, and receive a presentation by the party leader, or president. Listening to Paddy Ashdown, dealing patiently with our questions, I would often muse as to whether this was an effective use of the time of somebody who was obviously a very busy person. Peter Parker was obsessed with constitutional reform and would ask endless questions as to how policy was developing in this area. Paddy might be discussing foreign affairs or economic policy, but Peter would invariably chip in with 'don't forget constitutional reform'. He was suspicious of 'the two Tims', who, he thought, were anxious to avoid serious discussion, and too keen for us to rubber-stamp whatever came along. But, I suppose, they were also busy. Peter and I went, on one occasion, to their offices – they worked together – to pursue one line of enquiry on the party's finances, but it was inconclusive. I then volunteered to discuss matters with the accounting staff at its offices, but made little impact. The accounts were not consolidated, and there were various pockets of funds in different accounts. It was impossible to get a complete picture. Rather like the Police Federation's finances. I hope that things have improved.

One of the more interesting periods at the trustees meetings was in the run-up to the 1997 general election. Paddy had abandoned the long standing Liberal Democrat position of equidistance in its relationship with the other two parties. He was now having regular meetings with

Tony Blair, the Labour leader, about the possibility of a coalition government, in what was described as a uniting of the centre-left – the so-called 'progressive forces'. Paddy regaled us with details of his discussions with Blair. The Labour leader was a great enthusiast for the idea, but, we were told, his deputy, John Prescott, was spitting blood at the prospect. In the event, Labour's landslide victory meant that the project was aborted, but Paddy remained convinced that Blair would have preferred a different outcome. Paddy always saw himself as being on the radical wing of politics, very much in the Grimond tradition, and would never have countenanced any arrangement with the Conservative Party; but then neither could he have worked with 'Old Labour'. He was perhaps a little too easily beguiled by Blair. In recent years all of us, in our different ways, have had to make new accommodations.

At the occasional party dinners which I attended, I would invariably be placed next to Paddy, usually in the privileged position to his right. We had got to know each other, and I think that he was happier sitting next to somebody whose face he recognised, because, although I had made a modest financial contribution, I was certainly not a big donor. I was much more interested in trying to influence policy. Paddy was excellent on foreign affairs, and was a brilliant leader of a political party, but finance was not his strong point; and it was my main interest. I was concerned that the new party was too much under the control of its social democrat wing, and I wanted it to develop economic policies along traditional liberal lines – a smaller government and lower taxes.

I was unhappy with Paddy when he resigned, in January 1999, in circumstances which made it inevitable that

Charles Kennedy would succeed him as leader. Paddy and I have remained friends, I continue to be an admirer, and we have even spent a week skiing together (it is wise to keep out of his way on the piste) but he should have known better. Charles Kennedy was a lovely man with an easy charm, but he was not a liberal, had no interest in policy, knew little of economic matters, and had no organisational skills – his private office was chaotic (the private office malfunction is a charge now levelled at the leaders of all major parties; what they have in common is a lack of any managerial talent or experience – they have all spent virtually the whole of their working lives in politics.). I am afraid that Charles was a dilettante who just liked the idea of being leader; in much the same way as David Cameron likes being prime minister.

Whilst Paddy was leader, we had many exchanges of correspondence on policy matters, mainly on finance. He always responded at length, and in a thoughtful manner. In July 1998, I wrote to him to say that 'Liberal Democrats are seen to be uncritical supporters of the move to European Monetary Union, and as being critical of New Labour spending plans only on the basis that they should be bigger.' I added that 'I have long believed that the state is a bad, high cost, and inefficient provider of services.' Paddy did not react to the EMU point, but he made a long considered response on his approach to the funding of public services. He sent a further letter to me just before the 1998 party conference, which was more insightful. He said, 'There will be those who wish us to preserve and perhaps even sharpen our niche as the big spenders of politics. I shall oppose this ... tooth and nail, though whether I win depends as always on the conference vote.' He recognised, as I did, that the

Liberal Democrats were a democratic party, that the annual party conference was all powerful, and that most of its activists were not liberals, but social democrats.

In August 1999, when Charles was appointed, I wrote to congratulate him, to say that I looked forward to seeing him at the next trustees meeting, and to remind him that: 'I am an old-fashioned liberal who believes that governments do most things badly, and should do less.' The following year Charles was to publish a book in his name, which had been largely ghost-written. He asked me to read a draft and let him have comments. I read the book in one sitting – it took five hours – and made a mainly favourable response. However, in a fairly long letter – probably a mistake – I told him that 'overall I feel that the book is too timid.' I went on to say: 'Two of the most important issues which we face today, as you recognise, are education and health. Both can only be resolved satisfactorily by radical and revolutionary changes in the way in which they are financed and in the nature of their provision. But politicians of all parties shrink from facing up to the presentational problems which this might involve.' I concluded that: 'We desperately need a book which will approach the important issues of our time with intellectual rigour and without fear or prejudice. Is there still time for a re-think?'

Reading in now, it seems more than a little pompous, though I still strongly believe in its message, so it was perhaps not surprising that, despite a number of reminders, Charles did not respond. Charles Kennedy was not Paddy Ashdown. In fact, I assume that Charles was one of the people Paddy had in mind when he referred to the 'big spenders of politics'. Other candidates, from me at least, would have been the smug, over-rated Vince Cable and

159

the party conference darling, Shirley Williams. Both social democrats and no doubt proud of it; but not liberals. And the Liberal Democrats no longer seemed to me to be a liberal party. It was now producer led rather than consumer driven; on the side of health service professionals and the educational establishment rather than protecting the interests of patients and schoolchildren: the wrong side of the divide. It was new *Guardian*, whilst I was still old *Manchester Guardian*. I was also concerned about some of the unsavoury people who were now being encouraged to make financial contributions, with the expectation, if not actual promise, of reward – perhaps a seat in the House of Lords. In May 2001, I wrote to Peter Parker informing him of my decision to resign as a trustee. I said to him that 'I can no longer support the policies of the Liberal Democrats, or its present leader.'

As the 2005 general election approached, I again wanted to make a contribution to the political debate, despite no longer belonging to any political party. I wrote and published a pamphlet which I called a 'political rant,' and which was titled *Grumpy Old Liberal*. Just before the 2010 general election, I wrote a further polemic, *What Would a Liberal Do?* The first pamphlet had concluded that 'this grumpy, old, Manchester liberal will vote Conservative, and I urge fellow liberals – holding their noses if necessary – to do the same.' I have voted for the Conservative Party in subsequent elections, but still without any great enthusiasm. It remains very clear to me that I do not belong to that particular clan. I have drawn from both documents in writing parts of this chapter. I hope, in this different context, that it does not sound too shrill or strident.

When I co-authored *Counterblast* with Dennis Wrigley and Alan Share, I felt, as I have mentioned earlier, very much the junior partner. It was published in 1965, between the Accrington and Runcorn campaigns, and now, in 2005, I had gathered more confidence in my views and judgement. I felt that I had found my own voice. I had certainly had enough time. I re-read *Counterblast* to see how things had changed over this long period of 40 years – a working life-time – and how much they had remained the same, and *Grumpy Old Liberal* was the outcome.

'The West must concede,' we said in *Counterblast*, 'that during the last thirty years the philosophy that has dominated the world has been that of Communism, and, in recent years, Communism fused with Nationalism. The Communist has known what he wants and has gone forward to get it.' We quoted Dr Charles Malik, a former president of the UN General Assembly, who said:

> The West is too soft, too self-satisfied, too blind, too paralysed and anaesthetised morally, to act with vigour at the critical points in life and the world. A person, or a culture, or a civilisation, cannot rise above its inmost principals. In the Western world the principle is a higher and higher standard of living, more and more comfortable existence, nothing great, nothing historically profound. Nothing. That's why Communism seems to win everywhere. Because it seems to have something. You talk to a Communist and he believes in something. You talk to a Westerner, he believes in nothing.

Substitute the word Islam for Communism in all of the above and you might well feel that little has changed. And the Cold War, with which we had lived for so many years, has simply been replaced by the War on Terror. The collapse of the Soviet Union, the dismantling of the 'Evil Empire', and the disappearance of the Communist threat, happened with a suddenness which was astonishing. Had it all been exaggerated, I asked, in *Grumpy Old Liberal*, and were we now similarly exaggerating the new threat from Islam?

But the Soviet threat was real at that time. Those who lived through the Cuban missile crisis in 1962 will remember the feeling that we were on the brink of World War Three – and that this time it would be a nuclear war from which the world might never recover. Economically, the Soviet Union might have been a paper tiger, but this was not obvious at the time. Its possession of a large arsenal of nuclear weapons, and its apparent willingness to use them, even pre-emptively against a perceived threat to its own security, was a source of daily concern. It seemed that at any moment the Cold War might develop into a hot war, and our more paranoid neighbours became busy digging their nuclear bunkers, and laying down their food stores.

Communism did seem to be the new religion of the masses. Poor people throughout the world looked to Communism as their only hope of an escape from poverty. The reality of life under a brutal totalitarian regime was kept well hidden from potential converts. The Soviet Union offered aid and protection, which it could ill afford, to its new 'client' states, as the world was divided between two super powers and their respective spheres of influence. In the West, fellow travellers, and the cast of the usual suspects, Lenin's 'useful idiots', provided an intellectual cloak of fey respectability for this new form of exploitation, and for some of the more bizarre experiments in collectivisation which brought death and suffering to so many millions of people.

The Soviet Union would no doubt have imploded without external pressures as the sheer unworkability of its central control system fell apart. But, again, this was not clear at the time. The collapse, however, was accelerated by the inability of the USSR to bear the cost of the arms race with America, the final straw being 'Star Wars'.

The striking success of the free enterprise system, and in particular as exemplified by its more liberal Anglo-Saxon model (despite its many imperfections), cannot be overstated. The contrast with the Communist system which had combined a loss of individual freedom with total economic failure could no longer be gainsaid by even the most stubborn of those who had been the Soviet's cheer-leaders in the West. It is the unavoidable evidence of the West's, and more specifically America's, economic success, with its material rewards shown each day on television screens throughout the world, which is the provocation which now fuels the rage of Islam; or at least its more extreme elements.

Is the danger now of a new crusade? A world polarised between evangelical Christian fundamentalists and ex-tremist Muslim fanatics. A war of conflicting ideas with no room for tolerance. Has our complaint in *Counterblast* 50 years ago, that a society that believes in nothing is always at a disadvantage against those that believe in something, been answered? But not in the way we might have hoped; and, again, with liberalism being the loser. Or is the Islamic threat exaggerated, as I suggested might be the case, and the War on Terror misconceived?

The latest band of jihadists might be religious zealots pursuing their own brand of barbaric ideology, but it is more likely that they are simply depraved and deluded nihilists seeking their own 15 minutes of fame on television's 24 hour rolling news programmes. We have too often been too willing to give them the publicity which they crave. They are often people who are comically ignorant of the religious cause to which they are ostensibly committed, like the

163

convicted British terrorists, Mohamed Ahmed and Yusof Sarwar, who ordered from Amazon *Islam for Dummies* and *The Koran for Dummies*, before they left for their terrorist trip to Syria.

The Imams have been unforgivably slow in confronting those who distort their beliefs so heinously and with such catastrophic results. It is similar to the behaviour of the Catholic priests who were often reluctant to condemn the inhuman, unchristian, and criminal atrocities of the IRA. But, despite the dreadful horrors of Gaza, Syria, ISIS and the Ukraine, the last decade has seen fewer war deaths than any in the past 100 years. To give some kind of perspective, we should remember that 37 million people died in the First World War and 60 million in the Second. Every unnecessary death is a cause for personal grief, now heightened by the focus of television, but despite the apparent daily contradictions, including the massive over reaction to the recent Paris atrocities at *Charlie Hebdo*, we are living in the most peaceful era in history. There have always been misfits looking for a cause to which they can attach themselves and from which they can launch their own kind of mayhem. The present group of lunatics and gangsters are no more likely to succeed than the 'man in a cave' supposedly masterminding a world-wide terrorist network under the cloak of al-Qaeda.

Liberals should always give maximum support to humanitarian relief, whilst remaining deeply sceptical about any further involvement, unless there is an obvious identifiable threat to our own direct interests. However heart-breaking individual stories of horrific suffering might be, we are often incapable of making any constructive difference. Intervention has invariably failed, whether it is in Iraq, Libya or Afghanistan; it often makes things worse and can help to create new enemies.

In the next 50 years, we are far more likely to be looking for answers to problems which are expressed in Chinese characters, as the bamboo curtain goes the way of the iron curtain, and China inevitably moves into position as the world's second super-power, and the world comes to terms with a new bipolarity. But to return to Malik. Perhaps his analysis was not entirely right, because in the West, we do believe in something; in tolerance, in democracy, in individual freedom, and in the rule of law. We are just insufficiently vocal in spelling it out. We need to recover our self-confidence, and re-assert these values at every opportunity. It is the battle of words which we must win. We must show that the pen really is mightier than the sword.

In *Grumpy Old Liberal*, in 2005, I asked the question: 'Is it possible that Britain's long flirtation with Europe is about to end, and that it is no longer inevitable that Europe is the future?' My answer then, and even more emphatically today, is 'Yes'.

50 years ago, when we wrote *Counterblast*, Britain was often referred to as the new 'sick man of Europe' – in sharp contrast to the burgeoning economies of the countries within the new Western European bloc which had recently been formed, West Germany, France, the Benelux countries and Italy, the original members of the EEC. The European project sprang from a determination that the horrors of two world wars, which were still etched so clearly on the memories of its founding fathers, would not be repeated. Britain was excluded from these far-reaching developments. Initially, this exclusion was self -imposed, as, first the Labour government of 1950, and then the Conservative

government of 1951 refused to join the European Coal and Steel Community which was the precursor of what was to become the European Economic Community (EEC) under the Treaty of Rome in 1957, and then was to evolve into the European Union (EU). But when the Macmillan government, feeling that we might well have missed the boat to economic salvation, applied to join in 1961, Charles de Gaulle had great satisfaction in saying 'Non!' France was to veto a further British application from Harold Wilson's government in the late 1960s, and it was not until 1975, at the third time of asking, that Britain's application was finally accepted by Brussels, and sealed by the British public in the historic referendum campaign, which was supported by virtually all the 'great and the good' of the British political and business establishment.

The arguments for Britain's entry to the EEC were focused very much on the economic benefits of being part of a large and expanding market which was on our own doorstep; on trade and jobs. The very name which was then used to describe the EEC, the Common Market, epitomised this. Little was said about political union or European federalism. And the problems which the European project faces in Britain today have their roots in that referendum campaign of 1975. The original members of the EEC always saw it as a means of achieving complete economic and political union, bound by a single currency and a common constitution; more and more Europe; closer and closer together. The British electorate does not believe that this is what it signed up for.

Of course we should have read the Treaty of Rome. I didn't, and I have not met many who did. And those who did read it mostly kept quiet about it. People now make the obvious point, if somewhat belatedly, that the EU is undemocratic; they do not understand the argument. They should have read the Treaty. It was deliberately set up to frustrate the democratic will of its member states. The evils which had been visited upon the peoples of supposedly civilised and democratic Western European countries were still far too close. As Bruce Anderson has commented: 'They can hardly be blamed for concluding that nationalism comes in jackboots.' The EU does not plan to take any more risks with democracy; if a member state votes the 'wrong way' on any treaty change, then it must vote again until it provides the correct result. Our own traditions of parliamentary democracy do not chime with this.

As Brussels has accumulated more and more power, with each successive treaty, it has become a bureaucratic colossus which no liberal could support. The federalists see Europe in terms of protectionism and cross-subsidies rather than free trade and growth. The most notorious example is the Common Agricultural Policy (CAP), a ludicrously expensive sop to French farmers which effectively closes European markets to the producers in underdeveloped countries. Even such a Europhile as Tony Blair was forced to say, in a different context, 'You could not really care about Africa and defend the CAP.' Without the CAP, we would not need the same level of overseas aid. The countries of Africa would be able to trade freely with Europe, paying their own way, and enjoying greater independence and self-regard.

Europe is no longer the economic powerhouse it was when Britain joined. The insoluble problem of a single currency, without a unified state, and its illiberal policies of over-regulation and employment protection, are part of the problem; but a longer term issue is the demographics of a declining population and a significantly increasing ratio of pensioners to active workers. Britain's own demographics are not good, but Europe's are much worse. At a time when the rest of the world is showing strong growth in both population and gross national product, Europe is in long term decline.

For a liberal, a good test of any proposed government initiative is to ask, 'Is this something which can only be done by government?' If the answer is 'yes,' then he would ask if it could be better done by local government rather than by central government. The answer would hardly ever be Europe. Liberals believe that government should be kept to the necessary minimum, and that wherever possible it should be carried out locally rather than at the centre. In the nineteenth and early twentieth centuries, Britain was one of the most decentralised countries in the world with powerful local government and vibrant cities such as Liverpool and Manchester. Today it is one of the most centralised; and we now have the added burden of the EU. It is extraordinary that the Liberal Democrats should remain the EU's most fervent supporters when it flies in the face of liberal values. It is undemocratic, corrupt, illiberal, incompetent, protectionist, self-serving, stagnant, and seemingly incapable of reform.

We hardly need reminding that Europe is no longer a happy place. Germans do not like subsidising what they perceive to be the idle South; the Greeks, Portuguese and Italians do not like being told what to do by the Germans, and they all gang-up on the Brits for rocking the boat. There is a lack of trust and the fact that, within the Eurozone, people are not able to change things democratically poses obvious dangers; Greece is the latest example. Britain is now to have an in-out referendum on the EU, but David Cameron has compromised his negotiating position by saying that virtually regardless of the outcome he will recommend that we stay in. This is hardly likely to pressurise our European partners into making concessions which they will feel to be unnecessary. Mr. Cameron might return with a fig-leaf of changes, but I would be astonished if there is anything of substance. I have no doubt that it is now overwhelmingly in our national interest to withdraw from the European Union. There will be those who will say that millions of jobs will be affected as our trade with Europe is placed at risk: Exactly the same people who advocated our entry into the Exchange Rate Mechanism, and who claimed that our economic prospects would be ruined if we did not join the Euro. It is an outrageous suggestion which its proponents – with the Liberal Democrats at the forefront – disgracefully know to be untrue. The rest of Europe exports significantly more to Britain than we sell to it. There is a huge £50 billion trade surplus in its favour, and we are Germany's largest export market. It is ludicrous to pretend that the EU will not be at least as anxious as we are to negotiate new trading arrangements which will better suit us both. Freed from the straightjacket of the EU, we can then develop new trading links with the rest of the world where business is expanding, whilst the EU can get on with its federalising and trying to save the Euro. And then we can all be happy again; because when we have ceased the constant quarrelling which has been the feature of our membership, it will be easier to be friends.

Grumpy Old Liberal took a snapshot of an aspect of a British high street, which I believe remains valid today. A casual observer, I wrote, might see a pedestrian with a bottle of drinking water in one hand and a mobile telephone in the other, seeking to avoid stepping onto recently discarded chewing gum, whilst perhaps contemplating the purchase of a lottery ticket or a visit to a betting shop. In 1965, when *Counterblast* was published, bottled water and mobile phones did not exist as consumer products, and although chewing gum certainly did, there was no evidence of this on the pavements. People did not then eat or drink in the street, but appeared no less nourished or more dehydrated. To place a bet on a horse (other forms of gambling, apart from the football pools, hardly existed) the intrepid punter would have to go to a back-street bookmaker, usually approached through a urine-stinking back alley. Off-track gambling was then illegal. Today, there is a betting shop on every street corner (ironically and conveniently, often sitting next to a pay-day loan shop which is another new feature of the high street), where 50 years ago a public house might have been standing. Bottled water is now a major international commercial enterprise and people happily pay more per litre for water than for petrol, whilst at the same time complaining that the price of petrol is a national disgrace. Mobile telephones have become a fashion accessory which has invaded every part of our lives; anybody not owning one – I plead guilty – is thought to be an eccentric. The National Lottery, a clever device for transferring money from the poor to indulge the tastes of the rich, did not exist 50 years ago. And 50 years ago there was no Internet. Today one can order groceries on-line, and even the poorest families have a television set, sometimes two, and often with a flat screen and high definition.

Are people happier? It is a difficult question to answer. Britain is a much wealthier country but the increase in wealth has not been evenly distributed. The rich have grown richer at a faster rate than that at which the poor have become less poor. There has been an increase in inequality, and that has recently accelerated. An impartial observer from 1964 might judge that although most Britons are undoubtedly better off, they are less well educated, have poorer health care than that available in many comparable countries, are more badly and less democratically governed, have less control over their own lives, are less secure, and now face later retirement (cushioned by greater longevity), lower pension expectations, and great economic uncertainty. And Britain is more diverse. There are more immigrants; and most, at least in London, are younger, harder-working, better educated, and often speak better English, than their indigenous neighbours.

The increase in wealth has not followed a smooth and even trajectory. Far from it. For most of the first three decades of this 50 year period, Britain's economic performance was dismal. Regardless of the political complexion of the governing party, there was a continuation of the policy of managing gentle decline. It had earlier been described as 'Butskellism' by *The Economist*; a conflation of the policies of the Conservative chancellor, Rab Butler, and the Labour leader, Hugh Gaitskell. Wilson, who succeeded Gaitskell, suffered the humiliation of having to be rescued by the International Monetary Fund, and of devaluation (we still had fixed exchange rates), whilst claiming that the pound in our pocket was unaffected. His successor, Callaghan, eventually succumbed to the 'Winter of Discontent', when the dead lay unburied, the post was undelivered, and the refuse uncollected. Heath, who was the new Conservative prime minister, fell in his 'Who governs Britain?' election — the answer, apparently, was the miners. The connecting link between these events and the poor underlying economic performance was thought by many to be the trades unions, although timid management no doubt played a part. It was said that the unions were holding the country to ransom, and that their restrictive practices, guarded with particular ferocity by some of their more militant shop stewards, were preventing improvements in efficiency. All this was to change with the arrival of Margaret Thatcher.

'The opponents of almost every progressive measure which has been introduced in this country have always been found in the Conservative Party,' we said in *Counterblast*, in a paragraph headed 'The Reactionaries'. That harsh judgement might now be in need of some revision. There can be no doubt that Margaret Thatcher was the most radical, reforming prime minister for generations. Her abrasive manner (Michael Gove should take note) and seemingly uncaring side created many enemies, but the Thatcher government cut taxes (the top rate of income tax, which had been 83 per cent on earned income and 98 per cent on 'unearned' income, was reduced to 40 per cent), introduced laws which crucially broke the stranglehold which the trades unions then held on many parts of British industry, privatised public utilities, and preached a belief in free markets, competition, and the encouragement of entrepreneurship and individual responsibility. It is a pity that she failed to reform the core of the public sector, particularly health and education, and that she went on to concentrate, even further, power at the centre. And it is a scandal that she paid insufficient regard to those innocent victims who were adversely affected by her policies. But, subject to those important caveats, there is not much with which economic liberals could disagree.

The economic benefits of these changes were to be deferred by the catastrophic decision to join the Exchange Rate Mechanism (ERM). The establishment view on the economy, which conveniently meshed with its view on Europe, was that Britain's membership of the ERM – the precursor to the single exchange rate, the Euro – was a prerequisite for economic revival. The discipline of the ERM was put forward as the panacea to cure the twin evils of high inflation and high interest rates. The outcome was an overvalued currency, and even higher interest rates. It was an unmitigated disaster, the costs of which are measured not just in the enormous currency losses which were incurred at the time of our withdrawal, with Norman Lamont's humiliating statement on 'Black Wednesday' (it was 16 September 1992, and, on that one day, the Treasury lost more than £3 billion in the financial markets), but in the millions of jobs which were lost and the thousands of businesses which failed (I write from bitter experience) during the terrible recession which our membership had so cruelly exacerbated. When we were free from the constraints of the ERM, and our currency had adjusted to its appropriate market value, and when interest rates had returned to more normal levels, the Thatcher reforms meant that the conditions were in place for a transformation in our economic prospects. The outcome was a decade of uninterrupted growth, low interest rates, and low inflation. This was the economy which New Labour inherited. But Blair and Brown, claiming that the cycles of 'boom and bust' had been abolished, were to ruin it all with a programme of massive increases in public spending, from which we have still to recover.

To return to the phrase originally coined by Bill Clinton's campaign manager, James Carville, it's still 'the economy

173

stupid'. One of the problems of a democracy is that people are not told the truth. Politicians need to be re-elected. When we are told – correctly – that the deficit is being reduced, we assume that things are getting better. They are not, they are getting worse. It is impossible to exaggerate the disastrous nature of today's public finances. Total government debt is £1,500 billion (one and a half trillion pounds); it is £500 billion more than when Liam Byrne, then chief secretary to the Treasury, left his famous note to his successor to say 'I am afraid that there is no money left.' Despite government cuts in spending, which, because of the so-called 'ring-fenced' areas, have, in their totality, hardly yet begun to scratch the surface, borrowings are still increasing by almost £100 billion each year. If unfunded liabilities for public sector and state pensions and PFI contracts, which are not shown on the government's balance sheet, are included, then the total indebtedness is more than six trillion pounds, almost four times our gross domestic product, and the equivalent of £400,000 per average family.

If the government were a public company, it would long ago have been declared bankrupt. It has been operating a giant Ponzi scheme. In America, Bernie Madoff is in prison, serving several life sentences, for operating a similar scheme, but at a much more modest level. Today's pensioners are not being paid their pensions from a fund of the accumulated proceeds of their past contributions, but from today's taxpayers, and, increasingly, from debt. Longer life expectancy and changing demographics – more old people, and relatively fewer working – will add to the problem. Our grandchildren may well rebel against the profligacy and bad housekeeping of their grandparents when presented with the bill and told that there is no fund, and no money, just debt. We have been living beyond our means. That mantra cannot be repeated too often. And yet Britain's political parties still put forward their own pet versions of 'pork barrel' politics, spending money we do not have; offering new bribes to an increasingly sceptical electorate, and pursuing ludicrously expensive vanity projects such as HS2.

What Would a Liberal Do? was the title of my 2010 pamphlet. I will again attempt an answer. Liberalism espouses the fundamental British values, which were developed from traditional Judea-Christian teachings (I write this as a non-believer), of democracy, the rule of law, property rights, equality before the law, freedom of speech, and individual freedom, including the right to live free from persecution. It might read like motherhood and apple-pie, but sometimes the seemingly blindingly obvious needs restating, just because it is not always obvious to some.

It might be useful to reflect on how others have defined liberalism, and on the purpose of government. Millicent Fawcett, a leading suffragette and founder of Newnham College, Oxford, said: 'Liberalism means faith in the people, and confidence that they will manage their own affairs better than those affairs are likely to be managed for them by others.' Today half of what we earn is confiscated by government and spent on our behalf. We need to challenge the mind-set which believes that public spending is by definition a 'good thing'; a concept which has infected the entire political class. Liberals are sceptical of power, suspicious of the state, and put the highest value on individual liberty. Thomas Payne wrote: 'Government governs best which governs least.' The mediaeval jurist Henry de Bacton defined liberalism as: 'a framework of political institutions which makes limited government possible and effectively preserves the individual and his rights from invasion from above.'

Economic liberalism creates more wealth than any other economic model. Recently, Patrick Minford and Jiang Wang produced clear evidence to show that 'the surest way to increase economic growth is to reduce government spending and taxation'; and figures from the Organisation for Economic Co-operation and Development confirmed that an increase in public spending is directly linked to a decrease in growth rates. Social liberals can be seduced into believing that economic liberalism is harsh and uncaring; they then drift into the clammy embrace of the social democrats. They are wrong. They need to keep a clear head. The weakest and poorest in our society must be protected, but increasing taxes to pay for more public spending can be seen to be a self-defeating proposition. The only way we can pay for an even shrunken and reformed public sector is through economic growth; and it is only the encouragement of free enterprise which can produce that growth. Put another way, it is from the fruits of economic liberalism that we sow the seeds of social liberalism.

A diligent reader might by now have concluded that this liberal believes in low taxes, but with current government spending at £750 billion, whilst revenues are 'only' around £650 billion (the difference of £100 billion being added to government debt), tax reductions will have to wait. We can however look at our tax regime. Taxes should be simple, transparent, and easy to collect. The present system is a panoply of incentives, allowances, benefits, credits, and penalties which is beyond the understanding of most people, and which allows the unscrupulous – individuals and companies – to avoid paying their fair share (Gordon

Brown was proud of the fact that he had created so many more 'clients' of the State; in 1997, 700,000 households were in receipt of tax credits, but by 2010 it was 4.7 million; and the cost has risen from £1 billion to £30 billion).

I believe that the objective for a reform of income taxes should be a single flat tax rate and an abolition of all allowances (including, particularly, the tax relief for pension contributions which still costs £40 billion a year, and favours mainly the wealthy). A rate of about 30% on all incomes above, say, £12,500, should be roughly neutral in tax raising capacity (although, of course, the longer term objective should be to reduce the overall tax burden). There would be a need for temporary transitional arrangements, but the aim should be to remove the lower paid from the tax net, including national insurance, and help change a system where far too many people do not work because they receive more in benefits than they would earn, after tax, from employment. Ian Duncan Smith's proposals attempt to address one part of this problem, but they do appear to be highly complicated. The mansion tax was always a crazy idea – selecting just one category of asset classification (the same argument applies to the proposed rise in the inheritance tax threshold) – but a reform of council tax, with new higher bands to reflect the changes in house prices over the last three decades, would be a great idea, and could be used to help finance a re-invigorated local government.

The other major, adverse feature of our current tax system results from the highly centralised nature of our government. Around 90% of taxes in Britain are effectively raised and controlled by central government. In Switzerland, at the other end of the spectrum, a taxpayer would, typically, pay

20% of his direct taxes to the federal government, 40% to the canton (each canton also has its own regional bank), and 40% to his local town or commune. This means that the best local people in each community are attracted to joining its council, because it has real powers to take and spend their money. We need to move closer to the Swiss model.

Where do we start in seeking ways to reduce the £750 billion of government spending?

The biggest single cost of government is the cost of the people they employ. It often accounts for more than half of the total expenditure of a government department. A high, and increasing, proportion of that cost is in pension provision. A career civil servant, or local government officer (and each Member of Parliament), typically, has a pension entitlement equivalent to two and a half times that of a private sector worker. It should be obvious that this is unaffordable (the unfunded liability is already more than one trillion pounds) and new entrants should be offered conditions of employment which are closer to those in the private sector. We have a similar problem of affordability with the state pension. It is not the business of government to tell people when they should retire from work, but it is government's job to determine at what age they should receive retirement benefit. When state pensions were first introduced most workers never reached the age at which they were entitled to receive them. Even in the 1950s the average British male would receive a pension for only ten years; today it is for more than 20 years. The age at which people receive retirement benefits will need to be progressively increased, and it should also now be clear that we cannot afford annual above inflation increases for all (the triple lock) on state pensions.

The annual welfare bill is more than £220 billion. Liberals should have little difficulty in arguing that welfare should be restored to its original purpose of being a safety net and not a universal entitlement. Benefits should be concentrated on those in need, rather than being sprayed around to most families in Britain (Gordon Brown's 'clients'), including middle-class families. It is, for example, a nonsense that a £200 winter fuel allowance should be paid to the richest families in the land.

The other areas of ballooning expenditure have been health and education. It is not obvious that throwing more and more money at their problems has provided the answer.

The National Health Service, with 1.4 million people, is the world's third largest employer, after the Indian railways and the Chinese army. It has an annual budget of around £140 billion and is administered by its own army of bureaucrats at a cost of £5 billion. But the money will never, ever be enough; because the demand for health care is infinite, and the taxpayers' willingness or ability to fund it is not. Despite all the evidence to the contrary, with our cancer and stroke survival rates bottom of the OECD league tables, and a new scandal seemingly unfolding each day, there are those who perpetuate the myth that it is the envy of the world. A national treasure. They must be surprised that no other country has copied this uniquely British model. It is the last relic of the concept of the command economy. How many times do we have to show that it does not work; and how many more unnecessary deaths must we suffer? Yet for politicians of all parties it is politically toxic. They are afraid to offer the slightest criticism or hint of reform, and simply vie with each other in making false promises to spend increasingly mouth-watering amounts of money which we do not have. We need a system that is accountable to the people it serves (they exist elsewhere in Europe), and not to a centralised political establishment. A liberal would abolish the role of the state as a monopoly provider, provide greater choice for the patient, and review the concept of a universal health care system free at the point of delivery, whilst making proper provision for the poorest. With people living longer, and with new drugs increasingly expensive, there is no reason why those who can afford it should not make some contribution towards the costs of doctor and hospital visits and medication. But, at the very least, let us have a serious, open, and informed debate. There are alternatives.

The annual cost of educating our children is £100 billion. We have had poor value for money. In 2010, I wrote that if any floating voter wanted a single compelling reason for voting Conservative, then it could well be its education policy. I added 'this time the Conservative Party must not lose its nerve.' Britain's children are amongst the worst educated in the developed world, with too many leaving school without the basic skills of reading and writing and unable to perform simple adding and subtracting tasks without a calculator. Michael Gove seemed to be the answer; confronting the educational establishment, particularly the teaching unions, and giving a higher priority to the interests of parents and their children. He shares a belief that a combination of excellent teaching, unwavering attention to academic standards, firm discipline, high expectations, and inspirational leadership, can transform the life chances of all children, even those from deprived backgrounds – the education which grammar schools used to offer. Let's hope that the cowardice of David Cameron, and his apparent lack of any guiding principles, has not placed this at risk.

We need to continue the work which the brave Mr Gove has started.

A more radical approach to both health and education would be their wholesale privatisation. Those who could afford to (the vast majority, with dramatically reduced tax rates) would choose their own school and medical provider, and pay the bills directly, or more likely, by insurance. Or there could be a voucher system; there are many variables. There would be a cross-subsidy for the poorest from the taxes of the better-off. The aim would be to get government out of the way. But which politicians would propose that? Or even dare to think about it? It is all rather depressing.

The cost of a home is now well beyond the reach of most young families, particularly in London and the South East. In 1997 the average English home cost three times median salaries, today it is more than seven times (the price to earnings ratio in London is now 12.5). There is an obvious and severe imbalance between supply and demand, and the government's tinkering with the mortgage market, and introducing crack-pot gimmicks such as allowing already fortunate housing association tenants to purchase their homes with tax-payers money, simply pushes prices up even further without addressing the basic supply-side problem. We need to remove the barriers to housebuilding, confront nimbyism, relax the planning laws, and build more houses – many, many more; most should be in existing towns and cities where people and jobs are, and where services can be efficiently provided. When, in the 1950s and 60s we built 300,000 houses a year (today we build fewer than 120,000), half of them were council houses. Margaret Thatcher's programme of allowing tenants to purchase their homes on favourable terms, did not allow local authorities to retain the proceeds of those sales. They were unable to replenish their diminished stock. We should now give more powers to a stronger local government so that they can build new social housing for their more deprived residents, which, with the imaginative use of land brought forward for re-development, could be self-financing: Perhaps, this time, with fewer Le Corbusier-style tower blocks.

One area in which the government has been extremely lucky has been in the interest charges on our huge national debt. It currently amounts to around £40 billion a year, but it would have been much higher if it had not been for such a long period of artificially low rates of interest. And here is where it gets really scary. When quantitative easing unwinds – as one day it must – the consequences are entirely unpredictable. It is an experiment with the public finances which has not been tried before. But it is virtually inevitable that interest rates will rise, perhaps substantially. Every one per cent increase in rates would mean an extra cost to the exchequer of £15 billion. If rates were to return to close to their historic norm, then it would not be at all surprising if they were three per cent higher than today – an increase in the size of our interest bill of £45 billion. There has been little discussion of this in the recent election debates, but the pressure for further savings in other government departments, which this would imply, would be enormous.

A smaller state should mean a smaller government; fewer members of parliament, fewer cabinet ministers, and constitutional and electoral reform (a fairer voting system) which should result in a much reduced House of Lords, with more clearly defined powers. We need a more serious attack on Whitehall and its ministries, with whole government departments dismantled and abolished, with any remaining responsibilities absorbed by other departments (based on my own experience, a start could be made on the Department of Culture, Media and Sport, closely followed by the Department for Business, Innovation and Skills).

Many of us, at a time of austerity, must be mystified by the determination of all parties to 'ring-fence' the foreign aid budget, and insist on its meeting its target of spending 0.7 per cent of GDP – equivalent to about £11 billion, each year. Giving a minister an instruction to go out and spend more money is not usually a good idea. The money will not be spent wisely or efficiently. It might make politicians feel good, but it is a waste of scarce resources. The reform of the CAP would be a much more constructive approach to addressing the underlying poverty of much of the underdeveloped world. A smaller, more focused budget (only 8 per cent of the current aid budget is spent on humanitarian relief), could then be used for specific crises – such as the Nepalese earthquake – as they arise.

I suppose that I am an agnostic on climate change, but if there were a club for climate change deniers, then I would be tempted to join. What I find irritating, is the religious fervour and unbending certainty of the climate change activists. And it comes with a cost. Climate change policies increase household bills, adversely affect living standards throughout the world (but particularly in its poorest parts), and are responsible for obscenities such as the wind turbines which are a loss to the environment and a charge to the exchequer. Global temperatures may well have flatlined for a decade, and the science behind the theory of climate change is ambiguous. It is possible, as has happened throughout the history of the world, that underlying changes are taking place, but there are benefits as well as costs, and it is not entirely certain that they are net-harmful. What we should be doing is using our limited finances to deal with the potential consequences of climate change rather than seeking, Canute–like, to stand in its way. And please, please let's get on with fracking.

What would this liberal utopia look like? A reversal of the relentless accumulation of power and control by central government; a smaller more efficient state, with more functions, and tax raising powers, devolved to local communities, where government can be closer to the people it is serving; less emphasis on social engineering and more on wealth creation; lower and fairer taxes with the smallest incomes freed from tax; and a more self-sufficient and self-confident populace with a better housed and better educated workforce. The icing on the cake would be the stimulus to economic growth which a smaller state would produce; a richer, in every sense of the word, and more tolerant, country. And, of course, we would have left the European Union.

This, to put it mildly, might take some time to achieve. Five years ago, I wrote that it would take ten years to repair Britain's finances. The painfully slow rate of progress means that it will now take much longer. The fragile growth, about which the government is now trumpeting, is again built on the twin fault lines of increased debt (public and private), and inflated asset values (courtesy of quantitative easing). Many middle income families have been given a false sense of security by years of rock bottom interest rates, and they will face disaster when interest rates rise from their record low (total household debt is set to rise to £2.4 trillion, or 167 per cent of household income, by 2020). George Osborne boasts that we are doing better than our

European neighbours (in fact, if we use GDP per capita as the measure, adjusting for our large increase in population, rather than the crude unadjusted figure, then this is not the case as even 'basket-case' France is ahead of us). Nonetheless, giving Osborne the benefit of the doubt, my friend, Stephen Masty, recently drew the analogy of a bank of elevators all hurtling towards the ground, out of control, but with one falling a little more slowly than the others. Osborne was in the slower one; but it was still going to crash. He should be pressing the emergency button.

Jo Grimond wrote that 'there is no purpose in keeping a Liberal Party alive unless it promotes liberalism.' The Liberal Democrats are not a liberal party. They have rejected traditional free-market principles and now have their own version of democratic socialism; which is what Grimond so hated, but felt might be the Liberal Party's fate. It is typical that Liberal Democrats in government claimed success because they had slowed the pace and breadth of their coalition partner's reforming zeal. That is the problem. A liberal would have been pushing for more.

On May 7, 2015, I voted, again without enthusiasm, for the Conservative Party candidate for the third time in successive general elections. I do not feel comfortable supporting a party run by a small cabal of like-minded, privileged insiders with a sense of entitlement, but with little experience of the real world; a party financed by an equally small group of very wealthy businessmen. It is still the party of the rich, but for a liberal, there really was very little alternative.

It would have been difficult for a liberal to have supported the Labour Party. It is now an unashamedly socialist party, a believer in big government, and resistant to reform in the public services, particularly in health and education, but also in the police and fire services, all still under the control of Labour-friendly, public sector trades unions. It is still in denial about its responsibility for the ruinous legacy of its previous administration, and, regardless of the identity of its new leader, will never be weaned from its wealth-destroying tax and spend inclinations. It was George Osborne who said that you do not return the keys to the person who has just crashed the car. Osborne is in no position to lecture, as, when in opposition, he pledged to match Labour's spending plans, and promised further increases in public spending from a share in the proceeds of future economic growth; which proved somewhat illusory. On this issue, however, he is right. Labour, new or old, cannot be trusted to manage the nation's finances.

It would be wrong to say that I am disappointed with the leadership of David Cameron, because I never had any great expectations. In my 2010 pamphlet, I wrote that 'when the times call for giants, the land is inhabited by pygmies.' I thought it extraordinary that the Conservative Party had been hi-jacked by a Notting Hill clique with little experience outside politics, and with a leader whose only job away from the Westminster bubble was as a 'spin doctor' for a commercial television company. I added that 'Cameron and Osborne seem joined at the hip, with a taste for bullying rather than bravery being the defining characteristic.' Cameron's predecessor, Michael Howard, sent a furious letter to me saying, about Cameron, that 'you praise him in such faint terms.' I hadn't thought that I had praised him at all, but Howard is very protective of his protégé.

With Howard, who I thought to have been underrated, you knew pretty well where you stood. He was an economic liberal with traditional conservative views on social issues. Cameron claims to be a social liberal reformer, but on the role of the state in Britain today he has said little. Politicians are often poor managers, but at least they should have ideas. Cameron seems to fall short on both counts; reacting to events rather than seeking to shape them. Dr Charles Malik would not have approved. There is still a dislike of Cameron by many Conservative backbenchers, who complain of his arrogant manner and out-of-touch and un-collegiate style. But his surprising result in achieving an overall Conservative majority at the general election, despite his policy-lite campaign, means that we are now, almost certainly, stuck with him for another five years. I do not believe that he has the necessary conviction or energy to tackle the huge problems which face the nation. Of course, he no longer has the excuse that he is being held back by the Liberal Democrats. But I would not bet on him.

It is highly unlikely that any liberal would ever vote for the Scottish National Party or for the United Kingdom Independence Party. Yet, Alex Salmon and Nigel Farage have been the two most successful, populist politicians of their generation (I suppose we must now add Nicola Sturgeon to the list). All have been great communicators who have shown what passion and focus can achieve. And the SNP has shown that left-wing policies wrapped in a nationalist flag can still be electorally successful; if only there had been a Liberal voice to speak with the same conviction. I once spent an hour or two with Farage on the terrace of the Savile Club, where we smoked cigars and shared a bottle of wine. He is very good company, and, with good cause, he seriously hates and distrusts David Cameron. But, despite his persuasive powers (now perhaps on the wane), I find it impossible to take UKIP seriously as a political party. That view is strengthened by my slight acquaintance with some of its more prominent supporters. Cameron's use of the word 'fruitcakes' might have been ill-advised, but it was not too wide of the mark.

The two major elements in this most surprising of elections were the destruction of Labour in Scotland by the SNP, and the decapitation of the Liberal Democrats by the Conservative Party. Perhaps the most significant was the fate of the Liberal Democrats where the disaster was on a scale beyond contemplation. The number of seats is now down to eight, and the percentage of the poll is in single figures, which is where I came in with the old Liberal Party. But it is really much worse than that. To get another take on the magnitude of the calamity, I looked up the figures for Accrington (now Hyndburn), the constituency where I stood as the Liberal candidate in 1964. The share of the vote in 1964 (not a good year for the party nationally) was more than 13 per cent, in 2015 it was two per cent.

The Liberal Democrats lacked clarity. It is not enough to say that 'we will provide the brains for Labour and contribute compassion to the Conservatives.' But, in my view, it is the irreconcilable differences between the social democrat elements and the few remaining liberals which make it impossible to provide a coherent narrative. They will find it difficult to come back from this.

It was not long after the merger of the SDP and the Liberal Party in 1988 that I first began to have my own reservations. Most of the senior positions in the new party were occupied by former members of the SDP, who before that had been members of the Labour Party. Every political party is to some extent a coalition of different interests, but there has to be sufficient in common to bind them together. The statist tendencies and producer protective policies of the social democrats, as opposed to the free market principles and consumer friendly policies of the liberals, created an obvious problem; and the social democrat interest was now in the ascendancy. Paddy Ashdown did a reasonable job of managing the contradictory elements, but it has become more and more difficult. The election of Tim Farron as the new leader now makes this impossible.

I resigned from the Liberal Democrats in 2001. Paddy made one final attempt to get me back into the fold, some years later, when Ming Campbell was leader. He asked David Laws, who had succeeded Paddy as Member of Parliament for Yeovil, to invite me to lunch at the House of Commons, which he did. Vince Cable and Ed Davey were also there. Cable was taciturn, enigmatic, detached, possibly wondering why he was wasting his time. Davey was enthusiastic, eager to please, but perhaps a little naïve. Laws was earnestly intelligent. The odds against all three of them sitting in the cabinet, just a few years later, would have been in the stratosphere. I would certainly not have placed any of my money at risk, whatever the odds. I liked David Laws, and wrote to commiserate with him when he had his expenses problem, but I remained unmoved.

I do now wonder how much longer those active liberals still members of the Liberal Democrats, including former members of parliament such as David Laws and Jeremy Browne (both of whom might not thank me for this) think there is any point in fighting a battle they cannot win. Even the old Liberal Party never had a monopoly of liberalism. Roy Jenkins was a social liberal reformer as Labour home secretary, and Margaret Thatcher, of course, was a great economic liberal reformer. An influx of radically minded liberals into the Conservative Party, showing more enthusiasm than I have so far shown, could stiffen the resolve of like-minded economically liberal Conservatives. To return to the title of this chapter; that is what a liberal should do. Rather than applying the brakes to change, they could be pressing the accelerator.

X
TYING UP THE LOOSE ENDS

My poor grandmother was to die in the most tragic of circumstances. In January 1974, my Aunt Miriam and her husband, André, made a rare visit to Manchester to stay with my grandmother at her home in Cotefield Road. It was not quite a family reunion, but other family members came along for a festive evening – it was close to her ninetieth birthday. I was in Switzerland, with Barbara, on a skiing holiday. On the morning after the festivities, my grandmother was found dead, in her bed. Kathleen, who was the aunt who kept the family in touch with each other, decided that my holiday should not be interrupted, and I was not aware of what had happened until my return. I had missed the funeral, and I was desperately upset. It was typical Kathleen – trying to do everything for the best, but, on this occasion, she made a massive misjudgement.

Many years later, Kathleen said that she had a strange story to tell. André and Miriam were both unwell, and André had said to Kathleen, so she told me, that, if it seemed that Miriam was to become seriously incapacitated, then he would arrange for her death and that he would die with her; he could not live without her. I have done it once, he said, and I can do it again. When pressed to explain what he meant, André had said that, on the evening before my grandmother's death, he had deliberately given her an overdose of drugs. She was an old woman, he had claimed by way of an excuse, and had had a good innings. Kathleen was not sure whether he was fantasising or drunk, but she felt that she had to confide in me. Sometime later, Kathleen received a telephone call

191

from the police in Streatham. Miriam and André had been found dead together. The police had their suspicions, and a policeman came to interview Kathleen in Blackpool, where she was then living. But nothing further materialised, and the bodies were eventually released for burial.

My father died in 1979, in Wythenshawe Hospital, after a stroke. He was 66 years of age. In his later life, he had been drinking less, and had seemed a little happier and more at ease. He was proud of what he thought were my achievements and, if challenged about his occasional boasts, would show newspaper cuttings to his sceptical friends.

Kathleen, the last survivor of my father's siblings, died in 2006, when she was 88. She had been as poor as the proverbial church-mouse for the whole of her life, and had an impossible husband who would gamble away any money he could lay his hands on. Nevertheless, when I came to administer her estate, I found that she had squirrelled away significant sums of money in any number of bank accounts. Much of the family history died with Kathleen.

I had not been in touch with my brother, Alan, for many years, but we have recently re-established contact.

Barbara, as well as bringing up the three boys, devoted her home-building, gardening, and design skills into creating a new home in the Cotswolds. She sold more than one million copies of her cake books, which have been translated into more than 12 foreign languages.

Nicholas has established his own business in specialist motor car accessories; Anthony has pursued a career in bookselling, and is now the managing director of Stanfords; and Jeremy, after a time in Wall Street, is a successful restaurateur in New Jersey, and a ranked poker player. There are five grandchildren.

And for myself. I still ski five weeks each year, and play tennis at the weekends. I play bridge most days, in London, for what some consider to be high stakes. And I walk a lot. I walk in London, in the country, and also, in the summer, in Switzerland's Engadine valley. In the country, I walk with our dog, a schnautzer; there used to be three, including one called Dillon. I sometimes see deer, occasionally hare, and, even more rarely, perched on an overhanging branch by the pond, a kingfisher. The resident muntjaks are always around, and there is usually, though less often now, the urgent chatter of the sky-larks high up in the air. I might hear the pathetic squawking of a wounded pheasant, initially quite strong, and then fading like a battery running out of power; in the sky above, I hear the sharp screech of a buzzard as it circles the field and spots its next meal.

These sights and sounds and smells of the countryside I could hardly have imagined at 94, Viaduct Street. Every day, I realise how privileged I am, and how lucky I have been. But I would have given up everything for my mother to have lived longer, when I might have got to know her, and to have seen for myself what a good and generous person those who did know her told me she was. The mother to whose memory this book is dedicated, the mother I lost nearly 70 years ago, the mother I hardly knew.